OCCASIONAL PAPER 193

W9-CNX-159

Exchange Rate Regimes in an Increasingly Integrated World Economy

Michael Mussa, Paul Masson, Alexander Swoboda, Esteban Jadresic, Paolo Mauro, and Andrew Berg

INTERNATIONAL MONETARY FUND

Washington DC

2000

Production: IMF Graphics Section
Typesetting: Jack Federici
Figures: Theodore F. Peters, Jr.

Library of Congress Cataloging-in-Publication Data
Exchange rate regimes in an increasingly integrated world economy /
    Michael Mussa . . . [et al.].
        p.   cm. — (Occasional paper ; 193)
        Includes bibliographical references.
        ISBN 1-55775-892-1
    1. Foreign exchange.   2. Foreign exchange administration.
3. International economic relations.   I. Mussa, Michael.   II. International
Monetary Fund.   III. Occasional paper (International Monetary Fund) ;
no. 193.

HG3851 .E92 2000
332.4'5–dc21   00-035064

Price: US$20.00
(US$17.50 to full-time faculty members and
students at universities and colleges)

Please send orders to:
International Monetary Fund, Publication Services
700 19th Street, N.W., Washington, D.C. 20431, U.S.A.
Tel.: (202) 623-7430   Telefax: (202) 623-7201
E-mail: publications@imf.org
Internet: http://www.imf.org

recycled paper

Contents

Text Box

Text Tables

Text Figures

Appendix Tables

Appendix Figures

The following symbols have been used throughout this paper:

. . . to indicate that data are not available;

— to indicate that the figure is zero or less than half the final digit shown, or that the item does not exist;

– between years or months (e.g., 1994–95 or January–June) to indicate the years or months covered, including the beginning and ending years or months;

/ between years (e.g., 1994/95) to indicate a fiscal (financial) year.

"Billion" means a thousand million.

Minor discrepancies between constituent figures and totals are due to rounding.

The term "country," as used in this paper, does not in all cases refer to a territorial entity that is a state as understood by international law and practice; the term also covers some territorial entities that are not states, but for which statistical data are maintained and provided internationally on a separate and independent basis.

Preface

The exchange and payments crises of the 1990s, the general increase in capital mobility, and the boom-bust character of capital flows to developing countries raise anew the issue of appropriate exchange rate arrangements. This was recognized in the communiqué of the Interim Committee of the Board of Governors of the IMF of April 27, 1999, which asked the Executive Board "to consider further the issue of appropriate exchange rate arrangements, including in the context of large-scale official financing" (IMF, Press Release No. 99/15, p. 3). Responding to that request, this paper examines the consequences of heightened capital mobility and of the integration of developing economies in increasingly globalized goods and financial markets for the exchange rate regimes both of the world's major currencies and of developing and transition countries.

This paper builds upon previous studies prepared by IMF staff on various aspects of the exchange rate arrangements of IMF member countries, consistent with the IMF's role of surveillance over members' exchange rate policies and over the international monetary system. It has benefited from wide-ranging discussion at the Executive Board, as well as detailed comments from First Deputy Managing Director Stanley Fischer and other members of IMF management and staff. The views expressed in this paper are those of the authors and do not necessarily represent the views of Executive Directors or other members of IMF staff.

The authors are grateful to Freyan Panthaki and Haiyan Shi for research assistance and to Nahid Mejid and Maria Orihuela for secretarial assistance. Jaqueline Irving of the External Relations Department edited the paper, and Martha Bonilla and Gail Berre coordinated its production.

I Overview

The exchange rate regimes in today's international monetary and financial system, and the system itself, are profoundly different in conception and functioning from those envisaged at the 1944 meeting of Bretton Woods establishing the IMF and the World Bank. The conceptual foundation of that system was of fixed but adjustable exchange rates to avoid the undue volatility thought to characterize floating exchange rates and to prevent competitive depreciations, while permitting enough flexibility to adjust to fundamental disequilibrium under international supervision. Capital flows were expected to play only a limited role in financing payments imbalances and widespread use of controls would insulate the real economy from instability arising from short-term capital flows. Temporary official financing of payments imbalances, mainly through the IMF, would smooth the adjustment process and avoid undue disturbances to current accounts, trade flows, output, and employment.

In the current system, exchange rates among the major currencies fluctuate in response to market forces, with significant short-run volatility and occasional large medium-run swings. International private capital flows finance substantial current account imbalances, and fluctuations in these flows appear to be either a cause of major macroeconomic disturbances or an important channel through which they are transmitted to the international system. The industrial countries have generally abandoned control and emerging market economies have gradually moved away from them.

Three features of the modern international monetary and financial environment are particularly noteworthy. First, the revolution in telecommunications and information technology has dramatically lowered transaction costs in financial markets and spurred financial innovation and the liberalization and deregulation of domestic and international financial transactions. This, in turn, has facilitated further innovation and capital market integration. As a result, capital mobility has reached levels not matched since the heyday of the gold standard:[1] obstacles to trade in assets have been dramatically reduced and capital movements are highly sensitive to risk-adjusted yield differentials and to shifts in perception of risks. Financial markets have also become globalized in the sense that the balance sheets of major financial and industrial companies around the world are increasingly interconnected through currency and capital markets. As a result, shocks to important individual markets or countries tend to have greater systemic repercussions.

Second, developing countries have been increasingly drawn into the integrating world economy, in terms of both their trade in goods and services and in financial assets. As a consequence, these countries have been able to reap many of the benefits of globalization. However, they also have become more exposed to some of its risks and dangers, notably to abrupt reversals in capital flows. At the same time, private capital flows have come to play a dominant role in emerging economies' financing and adjustment.

Third, the emergence of the euro may mark the beginning of a trend toward a bi- or tri-polar currency system, away from reliance on the U.S. dollar as the system's dominant currency. An important issue is whether the exchange rates between major currencies will continue to exhibit the wide swings and occasional misalignments that characterized the 1980s and 1990s. This is an important issue for the system as a whole because such swings have important repercussions for third countries—developing countries, in particular. For the latter, a wide variety of exchange rate arrangements prevail, with a tendency to move toward increased exchange rate flexibility.

This paper examines the consequences of heightened capital mobility and of the integration of developing economies in increasingly globalized goods

---

[1]See, for instance, Obstfeld (1995b). A comparison with the pre-World War I gold standard period is complicated by very high labor migration, which has not been approached in the recent era, as well as strong cultural and political ties between the main lending country (the United Kingdom) and two of the largest recipients (Australia and Canada).

and financial markets for the exchange rate regimes both of the world's major currencies and of developing and transition countries. Section II discusses exchange rates of the major countries' currencies, and concludes that the exchange rates among the euro, the yen, and the dollar are likely to continue to exhibit significant volatility. (These currency areas are large and relatively closed, and Appendix I provides some evidence that such areas are likely to exhibit greater exchange rate volatility than small, relatively open, economies.) Section II also briefly examines various schemes to moderate such fluctuations, and concludes that these schemes are neither likely to be adopted, nor to be desirable under current circumstances, although a case can be made for monitoring potential major misalignments within the IMF's surveillance process. The section finishes with a discussion of key lessons from the experiences of the medium-sized industrial countries, whose exchange rate regimes, in an environment of increasing capital market integration, have moved increasingly toward either hard pegs (especially in the case of the participants in European Economic and Monetary Union—EMU) or to market-determined floating rates.

Section III reviews the economic environment facing developing and transition countries—including heightened capital mobility, continued exposure to exchange rate risk, increased openness to international trade, a shift of exports toward manufactures, greater intraregional trade, and lower inflation. It then considers lessons from the recent crises in emerging market countries, concluding that for developing countries with important linkages to modern global capital markets (as for industrial countries), the requirements for sustaining pegged exchange rate regimes have become significantly more demanding. For many emerging market countries, therefore, regimes that allow substantial exchange rate flexibility are probably desirable. Some emerging market countries, of course, may go in the other direction—toward hard currency pegs (such as currency boards), supported by the requisite policy discipline and institutional structures.

Beyond the emerging markets, for many developing countries with less linkage to global capital markets, the viability and suitability of exchange rate pegs is greater. This includes some of the larger developing countries, as well as a substantial number of smaller economies (see Appendix II). The few developing countries that still confront the problem of stabilizing from very high inflation may also find virtue in exchange-rate-based stabilization plans (see Appendix III), while giving due attention to timely implementation of an exit strategy. In contrast, several of the transition countries of Central and Eastern Europe, especially those preparing for membership in the European Union (EU) and participation in EMU, will want to establish over time the policy disciplines and institutional structures that support hard exchange rate pegs. Exchange regimes for developing countries in regional groups—notably the Association of Southeast Asian Nations (ASEAN) and the Southern Common Market (Mercosur)—with diversified trade linkages to industrial countries and important intraregional linkages raise particular problems, and a variety of potential solutions are examined. Before concluding, the section takes up important policies intimately connected with the exchange rate regime, emphasizing that countries adopting floating rates need a nominal anchor to secure the objective of low inflation.

Appendix IV reviews IMF advice to member countries on exchange rate arrangements. Consistent with the Articles of Agreement, the IMF's usual approach is to abide by a member's preferred exchange rate regime and to advise on policies needed to support that choice. Nevertheless, the IMF does sometimes question whether a country's exchange rate regime or the prevailing level of its exchange rate is consistent with the country's objectives and other policies. In the case of IMF-supported programs, the IMF lends to countries with exchange rate pegs only if its ex ante assessment is that such a policy is sustainable under the program, although there have been cases in which pegs subsequently had to be abandoned, typically in the context of policy slippages. In this regard, higher capital mobility makes more exacting the policy requirements for sustainability.

II Exchange Rate Regimes for Major Currencies

Since the creation of the IMF at Bretton Woods, the international exchange rate regime has undergone very substantial changes, which may be broken down into four main phases. The first was a phase of reconstruction and gradual reduction in inconvertibility of current account transactions under the aegis of the Marshall Plan and the European Payments Union, culminating in the return to current account convertibility by most industrial countries in 1958. The second phase corresponds to the heyday of the Bretton Woods system and was characterized by fixed, though adjustable, exchange rates, the partial removal of restrictions on capital account transactions in the industrial countries, a gold-dollar standard centered on the United States and its currency, and a periphery of developing country currencies that remained largely inconvertible. The end of convertibility of the dollar into gold in the summer of 1971 was a first step toward the breakdown of this system, which collapsed with the floating of major currencies in early 1973. This marked the beginning of the third phase.

During the third phase, the U.S. dollar remained firmly at the center of the system. The 1980s saw the gradual emergence of a European currency area, however, coupled with increasing capital market integration, and the 1990s witnessed the progressive drawing into an increasingly globalized economy of the developing countries and, with the collapse of the Soviet Union, of the transition economies. Many transition and developing countries put new emphasis on liberalizing their current account transactions. Capital mobility was increasing and globalization gradually took hold with the dramatic decrease in transaction costs associated with the telecommunications and information technology revolution and the attendant wave of financial innovations. Private capital flows came to play the major role in the financing of current account imbalances for many countries.

The exchange rate regime in the third phase was a mixed one. The currencies of the three largest industrial countries floated against each other and several medium-sized industrial countries' currencies also floated independently. At the same time, there were repeated attempts to limit exchange rate variability among various European Union countries, which culminated in the Exchange Rate Mechanism (ERM) of the European Monetary System (EMS) and ultimately in the creation of the euro. The dollar, however, remained by far the major international currency in both goods and asset trade. For developing and (later) transition countries, a mixture of exchange rate regimes prevailed, with a growing trend toward the adoption of more flexible exchange rate arrangements.

The birth of the euro at the beginning of 1999 may mark a fourth phase in the evolution of the postwar exchange rate system, a phase that will likely see an increasingly bi- or tri-polar system characterized by a high degree of capital mobility and a variety of exchange rate practices across countries. This section seeks to draw some lessons from the past in order to forecast the likely evolution and behavior of the exchange rate system for industrial countries over the next five to ten years. This analysis will also establish a basis for considering exchange regime issues for developing and transition countries that rely to a great extent on industrial country currencies for their international commerce and finance.

Trends in Exchange Rate Behavior

Over the past two decades, exchange rates of the major currencies—the U.S. dollar, the deutsche mark, and the Japanese yen—and those of other important industrial country currencies have exhibited substantial short-run volatility, large medium-term swings, and longer-term trends in exchange rates in nominal as well as real terms. Figure 2.1 illustrates this for five currencies and for the period extending from the first quarter of 1979 to the last quarter of 1998.[2]

Concerning short-term volatility, Table 2.1 reports that the standard deviation of quarterly changes in bilateral exchange rates of the deutsche mark, Japanese yen, French franc, and pound sterling against the U.S. dollar stands at between 5 percent and 6 per-

---

[2]Figure 2.1 and Table 2.1 also contain data for an index of a synthetic euro that will be referred to later in the text.

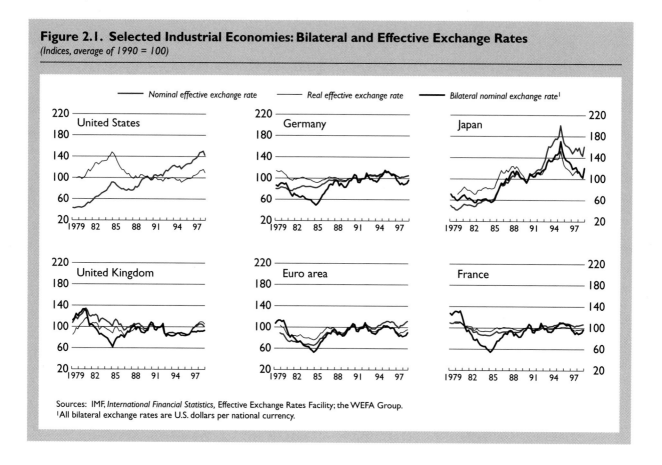

Figure 2.1. Selected Industrial Economies: Bilateral and Effective Exchange Rates
(Indices, average of 1990 = 100)

Sources: IMF, *International Financial Statistics*, Effective Exchange Rates Facility; the WEFA Group.
¹All bilateral exchange rates are U.S. dollars per national currency.

cent. The volatility of nominal and real *effective* exchange rates is also high although generally significantly lower than it is for the bilateral rates. Nominal exchange rate volatility is considerably higher than it was under the Bretton Woods system prevailing from 1945 to 1971 when, aside from a few exchange rate adjustments, standard deviations of quarterly changes in bilateral (and effective) nominal rates were essentially zero.

Medium-term swings in exchange rates have also been quite large, especially for nominal bilateral rates, as is apparent from Figure 2.1. They include, among others, the 1980–85 appreciation of the dollar followed by its subsequent depreciation over the next two years, and the 1990–95 appreciation of the yen followed by its sharp depreciation until mid-1998. These swings are also apparent in the extent of the range between the maximum and minimum values of the various indices. For example, the bilateral nominal index for the deutsche mark stood at 86.9 for the first quarter of 1979 and ended at 97.0 in the last quarter of 1998—a modest appreciation for the period as a whole—but it ranged from a high of 115.5 to a low of 49.5, a range of more than 130 percent. These medium-term swings appear also, but

more mildly, in nominal and real effective exchange rates. There are also (generally) mild longer-run trends in real effective exchange rates. The trend average quarterly real effective appreciation is 0.13 percent for the deutsche mark and –0.03 for the French franc; that for the Japanese yen at 0.70 percent is significantly higher. The causes of such longer-term trends in real effective exchange rates, whether attributable to so-called Balassa-Samuelson productivity effects, to measurement problems, or to other causes have been widely discussed in the literature and need not be taken up here.[3]

Of these characteristics of the behavior of major currency exchange rates, the greatest concern has focused on their large medium-term movements, especially among the currencies of Germany (together with most of continental Europe), Japan, and the United States. Wide swings in these exchange rates have on occasion been identified with "misalignments" and have given rise to questions of whether and how they can be avoided, or at least moderated.

---

[3]See, among others, Balassa (1964), Samuelson (1964), and Isard and Symansky (1996).

Table 2.1. Selected Industrial Economies: Volatility of Bilateral and Effective Exchange Rates, 1980/II–1998/IV

(In percent)

	Bilateral Versus U.S. dollar[1]	Nominal Effective Exchange Rate[2]	Real Effective Exchange Rate[2]
Germany			
Standard deviation of quarterly changes	5.26	1.63	1.69
Trend quarterly appreciation[3]	0.72	0.47	0.13
Japan			
Standard deviation of quarterly changes	5.70	4.78	4.69
Trend quarterly appreciation[3]	1.28	1.98	0.70
France			
Standard deviation of quarterly changes	5.14	1.62	1.54
Trend quarterly appreciation[3]	0.30	0.19	−0.03
United Kingdom			
Standard deviation of quarterly changes	5.23	3.62	3.85
Trend quarterly appreciation[3]	−0.12	−0.42	−0.13
United States			
Standard deviation of quarterly changes	...	3.14	3.10
Trend quarterly appreciation[3]	...	1.39	−0.30
Euro area			
Standard deviation of quarterly changes	5.01	3.00	2.96
Trend quarterly appreciation[3]	0.35	0.67	0.21

Sources: IMF, *International Financial Statistics*, and Information Notice System; the WEFA Group.

[1]All bilateral exchange rates are U.S. dollar per national currency.

[2]Effective exchange rates are trade-weighted indices; the real effective exchange rate is based on the consumer price index.

[3]Based on a regression of the natural logarithm of the level of the exchange rate on a time trend.

The recent movements in the value of the yen and the advent of the euro have given added weight to these concerns.[4] Although exchange rate fluctuations are often equilibrating or reflect diverging cyclical positions or monetary policies, it seems likely that at least some large exchange rate movements for both advanced countries and emerging markets do not plausibly reflect economic fundamentals.[5] Three questions arise in the context of the key currencies. First, is there any evidence that the volatility of exchange rates has changed over time? Second, can one expect the dollar/euro exchange rate to be relatively stable? Third, what are the medium-run prospects for more active management of the major currency exchange rates?

On the first of these questions, Figure 2.1 suggests that one can find periods of greater and periods of lesser volatility, and possibly that volatility was higher at the beginning and again toward the end of the period extending from 1979 to 1998. This may be the case over relatively brief periods, but volatility does not follow any particular trend. Table 2.2 shows the pattern of standard deviations of the monthly growth rates of nominal and real bilateral (against the U.S. dollar) exchange rates of 12 currencies and of a synthetic euro, as well as by that of their effective counterparts, for the period June 1973 to November 1998 and three subperiods of equal length. As can be seen in the table, the near equality of standard deviations across subperiods is so striking that a formal statistical test of this fact is redundant.[6] As could be expected, standard deviations of effective rates tend to be lower than those of bilateral rates.

---

[4]Surveys of the literature on the effects of exchange rate volatility on trade and investment are presented in IMF (1984) and Edison and Melvin (1990). For more recent results and discussions, see Commission of the European Communities (1990), Gagnon (1993), Frankel and Wei (1993), Frankel (1997), Dell'Ariccia (1998), and Eichengreen (1998).

[5]Flood and Rose (1995), for instance, are unable to find any (linear) relationship between exchange rate movements and a set of plausible macroeconomic fundamentals.

[6]Division of the sample period into two, four, and five subperiods yields similar conclusions. The results in Table 2.2 are based on period-average measures of the nominal exchange rate, since end-of-period data for the real and effective exchange rates, as well as for the nominal value of the synthetic euro, were not readily available. However, standard deviations of growth rates of end-of-period nominal bilateral exchange rates against the U.S. dollar (except for the synthetic euro) were also calculated. They are higher, as expected, than those reported in Table 2.2 but, like the latter, are quite similar across subperiods.

Table 2.2. Selected Industrial Economies: Volatility[1] of Monthly Bilateral and Effective Exchange Rates, 1973–98

(In percent)

	Bilateral Rate Versus U.S. dollar[2]		Effective Exchange Rate[3]			Bilateral Rate Versus U.S. dollar[2]		Effective Exchange Rate[3]	
	Nominal	Real	Nominal	Real		Nominal	Real	Nominal	Real
Australian dollar					**Japanese yen**				
Whole sample	2.3	2.3	2.4	2.3	Whole sample	2.9	2.9	2.5	2.5
First third	2.0	1.9	2.1	2.2	First third	2.6	2.5	2.3	2.4
Second third	2.8	2.8	2.6	2.6	Second third	3.0	3.1	2.5	2.3
Third third	2.0	2.0	2.2	2.2	Third third	3.1	3.2	2.8	2.8
Belgian franc					**Dutch guilder**				
Whole sample	2.7	2.5	0.8	0.8	Whole sample	2.7	2.5	0.7	0.7
First third	2.7	2.0	1.0	1.0	First third	2.7	2.0	0.8	0.8
Second third	3.0	2.9	0.6	0.6	Second third	2.9	2.9	0.7	0.7
Third third	2.6	2.6	0.8	0.8	Third third	2.6	2.7	0.7	0.7
Canadian dollar					**Swedish kronor**				
Whole sample	1.0	1.1	1.2	1.3	Whole sample	2.5	2.4	1.5	1.6
First third	1.0	1.0	1.0	1.1	First third	2.3	1.6	1.6	1.7
Second third	1.0	1.0	1.3	1.4	Second third	2.5	2.5	0.4	0.7
Third third	1.0	1.1	1.2	1.2	Third third	2.8	2.9	2.0	2.0
Finnish markkaa					**Swiss franc**				
Whole sample	2.5	2.5	1.4	1.4	Whole sample	3.1	2.9	1.4	1.4
First third	1.8	1.5	0.9	1.0	First third	3.1	2.5	1.5	1.4
Second third	2.7	2.7	1.2	1.2	Second third	3.3	3.2	1.2	1.2
Third third	2.9	2.9	1.8	1.8	Third third	3.0	3.0	1.4	1.4
French franc					**British pound**				
Whole sample	2.7	2.4	0.9	0.9	Whole sample	2.6	2.6	1.8	1.9
First third	2.6	1.9	1.0	1.1	First third	2.4	2.2	2.0	2.2
Second third	2.9	2.9	0.7	0.6	Second third	2.8	3.0	1.6	1.7
Third third	2.5	2.5	0.8	0.8	Third third	2.6	2.6	1.9	1.9
Deutsche mark					**U.S. dollar**				
Whole sample	2.8	2.5	0.9	0.9	Whole sample	...	...	1.7	1.7
First third	2.9	2.0	1.0	1.0	First third	...	...	1.7	1.9
Second third	2.9	2.9	0.8	0.8	Second third	...	...	1.7	1.6
Third third	2.6	2.6	0.9	0.9	Third third	...	...	1.4	1.4
Italian lira					**Synthetic euro**				
Whole sample	2.6	2.4	1.4	1.4	Whole sample	2.6	2.6	1.6	1.6
First third	2.5	1.7	0.7	0.8	First third	2.4	2.7	1.7	1.8
Second third	2.6	2.6	0.6	0.9	Second third	2.8	2.7	1.5	1.5
Third third	2.7	2.7	2.1	2.1	Third third	2.5	2.5	1.4	1.4

Sources: IMF, *International Financial Statistics*, and Information Notice System; WEFA.

[1] Volatility is measured by the standard deviation of the monthly growth rate (defined as the difference of the natural logarithm multiplied by 100) of the series.

[2] The series are monthly from June 1973 to December 1998 except for the real euro rate, which starts in January 1979. The real exchange rate is based on the consumer price index.

[3] The effective exchange rate series are monthly from February 1979 to December 1998 with the following exceptions. The synthetic euro rate, the Japanese yen real rate and the Italian lira real rate start in February 1980 while the Australian dollar real rate, the French franc real rate, and the U.S. dollar real rate start in January 1980. The real effective exchange rate is based on the consumer price index.

On the second question, the likely future behavior of the euro, it is useful to begin by considering the past behavior of a synthetic euro—that is, an index of the exchange value of a composite of the 11 currencies that compose the new European currency. Note that the trade weights used to construct the bilateral and effective exchange rates for the synthetic euro relate only to trade with countries outside of the euro area. The behavior of these synthetic exchange rates is shown in the euro panel of Figure 2.1 (and in Table 2.1). The data indicate that the behavior of the bilateral nominal exchange rate of the synthetic euro is quite similar to that of the deutsche mark, the French franc, and other continental European currencies closely linked to the deutsche mark, as appears also broadly true for the euro's effective rates (which, however, show a slightly larger variability than the mark does).[7] One important reason for the relatively high variability of the synthetic euro in the past, and for the likelihood that it will continue to be relatively high in the future, is that the euro exhibits the type of high variability in either nominal or effective terms that is typical of the currency of a large country (or group of countries with tightly linked currencies) relative to that of a smaller, more open economy that typically has higher trade volumes relative to GDP. Appendix I presents some evidence supporting this hypothesis.

The consistency of the synthetic euro's volatility across subperiods with substantially differing economic conditions and policies, in the euro area countries and outside, provides the basis for a reasonable forecast of the actual euro's volatility. There are also reasons to believe that the actual euro's volatility might be either modestly higher or modestly lower than that which has characterized the synthetic euro.[8] On the higher side, some of the past monetary shocks in individual countries of the euro zone have,

to some extent, offset one another and thus have contributed to making the bilateral dollar exchange rate of the synthetic euro more stable than that of, say, the deutsche mark. Also, although the introduction of the euro did not alter the degree of openness of the euro area vis-à-vis the rest of the world, the euro area is less open than the economies of its participants are. This may mean that the monetary policy of the European Central Bank (ECB) will be less sensitive, directly or indirectly, to exchange rate fluctuations vis-à-vis the rest of the world than were the monetary policies of its predecessor national central banks. On the lower side, we may see more stable monetary policy on the part of the ECB than that of the previous average of the euro area's component policies, coupled with similar stability in the United States. Moreover, the development of broad and resilient markets for short-term instruments denominated in euros may facilitate stabilizing speculation. The prudent conclusion, however, remains that one should not expect significantly lower volatility in euro exchange rates than that which has been exhibited by its synthetic counterpart in the past.

Exchange Rate Regimes for Major Currencies: Some Issues

The remaining question is whether a major policy initiative aiming at stabilizing the euro/yen/dollar triplet (the Group of Three G–3 currencies), is warranted or likely. There are two fundamental reasons for seeking to stabilize the G–3 triplet: the harmful effects of large medium-term swings in the value of these three currencies on the European, Japanese, and American economies; and the adverse effects of such swings on the economies of third countries, including in the developing world.

To what extent do large, medium-term swings in G–3 exchange rates represent "misalignments" that might have untoward consequences for the allocation of resources and for macroeconomic stability? This question has been discussed in two chapters of a recent paper by IMF staff (Isard and Faruqee, 1998), "A Methodology for Exchange Rate Assessments" and "Application in Fund Surveillance over Major Industrial Countries," which describe an approach employed by the staff's Coordinating Group on Exchange Rate Issues (CGER). The CGER methodology begins by estimating a country's underlying current account, that is, the current account that would result if prevailing real effective exchange rates remained unchanged and if all countries moved to potential output over a medium-run horizon. It then estimates the "normal" saving-investment balance that would prevail at the same

---

[7]The higher trend appreciation of the euro's effective exchange rate as compared with that of the mark may appear puzzling at first. The puzzle disappears when one remembers that the exchange rate for the synthetic euro excludes intra-area trade. Consider the following simple and deliberately unrealistic numerical example. Assume a world made up exclusively of three identical countries and three currencies: the deutsche mark, the French franc, and the U.S. dollar. Let the trade weights assigned to the deutsche mark/franc and the deutsche mark/dollar rate be equal to each other and to 50 percent. Let the deutsche mark appreciate by 1 percent against the franc and by 3 percent against the dollar; in effective terms, the deutsche mark appreciates by 2 percent. Then, let France and Germany be the euro area, which trades only with the United States. Under this scenario, the synthetic euro appreciates by 2.5 percent in effective terms. This is because the franc, which comprises 50 percent of the index, appreciates by 2 percent against the dollar, and the deutsche mark, which accounts for the remaining 50 percent, appreciates by 3 percent against the dollar.

[8]This question was discussed in contributions by Cohen (1997) and by Bénassy-Quéré, Mojon, and Pisani-Ferry (1997) at a conference held at the IMF on *EMU and the International Monetary System.*

horizon. The latter estimate, which is derived independently of the exchange rate, is then compared with the former estimate, and the real exchange rate that would be required to bring the underlying current account into equality with the normal saving-investment balance is calculated. If that medium-term equilibrium exchange rate differs widely from current exchange rates (say, by more than 10–15 percent, to recognize the imprecision that necessarily attaches to this type of exercise), a judgement is formed on whether and in what sense the difference can be considered a misalignment.[9] Both this and other methods for detecting discrepancies between current and equilibrium values of exchange rates would label a number of recent episodes as "misalignments." Among those, the pattern of major exchange rates that prevailed in early 1985, the pattern of exchange rates that prevailed among a number of European currencies in early 1992, and the relationship between an overvalued yen and undervalued dollar of early 1995 figure prominently.[10]

The CGER methodology clearly has its limitations. Diagnosing the source of misalignments and drawing out their policy implications is both more difficult and more controversial than identifying a discrepancy between some necessarily normative, or model-bound, concept of an equilibrium exchange rate and current exchange rates. Isard and Faruqee (1998, p. 2) provide a convenient, brief summary of alternative views of the usefulness of calculating equilibrium exchange rates and evaluating whether currency values may have become "misaligned." According to one view, current exchange rates always reflect fundamentals (which, themselves may be out of kilter, however) and can never be misaligned in a meaningful sense. A second view holds that, even though exchange rates may conceivably become misaligned, it is virtually impossible to identify such instances with any confidence, in practice. According to a third point of view, that of the authors of the IMF study and of this paper, quantitative assessment of instances of discrepancies between current and medium-term equilibrium exchange rates is useful and can provide a valuable input into policy evaluation. Ascertaining such a discrepancy, however, does not necessarily mean that exchange rates are misaligned: understanding the reasons for the discrepancy is critical. Thus, the pre-

vailing exchange rate may be appropriate even though it differs from its estimated medium-term equilibrium level if, for instance, the discrepancy reflects cyclical factors. Alternatively, the discrepancy may reflect misaligned policies rather than misaligned exchange rates, calling for a change in policies. Finally, there are cases where policies are appropriate but exchange rates are inappropriate, essentially because investors misjudge the policy stance. This would call for an effort on the part of the relevant authorities to influence incorrect market perceptions.

Views on whether how and to what extent it might be desirable to attempt to stabilize the exchange rates of major industrial countries differ widely. These views range from advocacy of a pure float, a view espoused especially by those who believe that exchange rates always reflect fundamentals and/or that the authorities do not possess knowledge superior to that of the market in such matters,[11] to proposals for the creation of a world currency. Intermediate proposals include target zones of the type suggested by Williamson (1985),[12] a quasi-fixed exchange rate regime among the G–3 to be achieved by monetary policy rules aimed at the exchange rate (McKinnon, 1996), a "virtual" Asian dollar peg (McKinnon, 1999), and various schemes for policy coordination that would take the exchange rate into account. Recent calls by some German and French policymakers for stabilization of the central triplet of currencies, along the lines of a target-zone type arrangement, have lent renewed interest to such schemes.

There are two basic objections under current circumstances to any scheme that would attempt to achieve substantial fixity of exchange rates among the euro, yen, and dollar. The first is that it would require largely devoting monetary policy in the three regions (or, more precisely, in at least two of them) to the requirements of external balance. To the extent that these requirements conflict with the domestic objectives that would otherwise dominate the determination of monetary policy, there could be very important costs from such a shift in monetary policy objectives in the major currency areas. Indeed, the fact that movements of exchange rates among the major currencies have, on many occasions, reflected divergences in relative cyclical positions and in the differential patterns of monetary policies needed to achieve reasonable price stability and support sustainable growth suggests that this concern is warranted.

---

[9]The estimates are derived, in an internationally consistent framework, for industrialized countries only, for data availability reasons and as the methodology assumes that countries have unrestricted access to international capital markets. The methodology also attempts to take cyclical and expectational factors into account. See Isard and Mussa (1998), Chapter 2 in the preceding publication, for a detailed account.

[10]These are the examples given in Isard and Faruqee (1998).

---

[11]For a cogent defense of this view, see Feldstein (1988).

[12]See also Williamson (1994) and Williamson and Miller (1987).

Second, the three regions do not conform to the usual criteria for an optimum currency area,[13] making the whole arrangement exceedingly vulnerable to asymmetric shocks as long as prices and wages are not fully flexible. The past decade has highlighted the lack of synchronization in economic activity in the three regions, and there is no reason to believe that differences across them would not prevail in the future. And, although Europe may be the region with the most evident labor flexibility problems, neither the economies of Japan nor the United States are likely to have sufficient real wage flexibility to adjust to large equilibrium movements in relative wages among G–3 countries without nominal exchange rate flexibility. In view of these objections and in the absence of the type of political commitment that accompanied the euro's introduction, any attempt at fixing the exchange rates of the triplet would lack credibility and would be rapidly undone by the market.

Looser forms of exchange rate stabilization, such as some variant of the target zone scheme originally proposed by Williamson, could also be envisioned. However, lack of political commitment and a number of technical difficulties would probably defeat the more ambitious, "harder," versions of the target zone schemes. Early versions of the target zone proposal were fraught with difficulties, in particular their partial equilibrium nature and their assumption that a number of real variables (e.g., real interest rates) could be attained through nominal (mainly monetary) policies. Later versions remove some of these flaws but serious problems remain. The calculation of the fundamental equilibrium real exchange rate poses conceptual and practical difficulties. There are insufficient instruments to hit the targets, given that the real exchange rate is an endogenous variable in the medium to long term and cannot be controlled by monetary instruments. And such schemes are at least as demanding of international macroeconomic cooperation as are more traditional attempts to manage nominal exchange rates.

It is difficult to imagine that the less ambitious, "softer" target zone proposals—with their very large and unannounced bands, adjustable parities, and scant policy commitments—would provide the transparency and the firm foundation for policies needed to avoid conflicts and anchor expectations. Even such looser arrangements would be unlikely to prove durable in the face of domestic economic circumstances calling for economic policies in the G–3 countries that are inconsistent with exchange rate commitments. Moreover, it is hard to see the overall

benefit in directing key macroeconomic policies (especially monetary policies) to achieve greater exchange rate stability among the G–3 if this entails greater domestic economic instability.[14]

Two points may be made to conclude this subsection. First, stability of major currencies' exchange rates does entail important external benefits for third countries, and instability entails important costs. Even if the direct effect of exchange rate volatility on net trade volumes is generally fairly small,[15] large exchange rate swings between close trading partners may create substantial sectoral adjustment costs. There is thus a positive externality for the periphery in good management of the exchange rate regime at the core. Indeed, the surveillance mandate of the IMF gives it a responsibility in this respect. Both multilateral surveillance and the bilateral surveillance of Article IV consultations are needed to pay appropriate attention to the domestic and international implications of major currency exchange rates and of related economic policies.

Second, over the medium term, the current group of euro zone countries is likely to expand, notably to admit new members in central and eastern Europe. At the same time, a significant group of countries will continue to peg their currencies to or closely follow the dollar. At present, it appears less likely that a zone will emerge with the yen as a single anchor and key currency. The prospects for an enhanced international role for the yen hinge on a sustained and vigorous recovery of the Japanese economy and on the success of continuing efforts to foster deeper, more innovative capital markets. As discussed in Section III, regional currency areas may emerge in Asia over a longer horizon, notably among the ASEAN countries, and the yen could conceivably play an important role in such arrangements. In this world of large currency areas, where exchange rate fluctuations impinge on a significant share of world trade in goods and assets, multilateral surveillance of exchange rate arrangements and related policies will be particularly important.

---

[13]These criteria are discussed in Section III.

[14]When the IMF staff extensively considered the issue of target zones and other proposals for stabilizing exchange rates among major currencies in 1994 (see Mussa and others, 1994), it reached essentially the same conclusions as in this paper. Such proposals are generally not desirable because they would require diverting key macroeconomic policies in the largest economies from their critical domestic stabilization objectives. And, for this same reason, such proposals are unlikely to be adopted.

[15]Eichengreen (1998) concludes that a growing consensus is emerging that the effect of exchange rate volatility on trade volumes, while significant, is small. See also Frankel (1997) for a discussion. Crockett and Goldstein (1987) contains an earlier analysis of these issues.

Experience with the Exchange Rate Regimes of Medium-Sized Industrial Countries

Although floating rates have characterized the exchange rate regime among the world's three most important currencies for more than a quarter century, regimes for the currencies of medium-sized industrial countries have been more varied, across countries and over time.[16] It is useful to reflect on this experience both for what it suggests for future exchange regimes of these countries and for the lessons it may teach concerning exchange regimes for emerging market and developing countries.

First, pegged exchange rate regimes have been used over extended periods by many medium-sized industrial countries, and these regimes appear to have functioned reasonably well in several instances. At one extreme, Luxembourg maintained a monetary union with Belgium from 1916 until the introduction of the euro at the beginning of this year. On a less rigid basis, Austria, Belgium, Denmark, and the Netherlands established and maintained tight pegs to the deutsche mark for a number of years in the ERM of the EMS. Maintenance of these exchange rate pegs generally required the subordination of domestic monetary policies to the policy of the Deutsche Bundesbank. In some circumstances, this may have meant that monetary policy was less well attuned to domestic economic objectives than might otherwise have been possible. On the other hand, during periods of turbulence such as the ERM crises of 1992–93, the exchange rates of the Austrian schilling and the Dutch guilder to the deutsche mark did not come under heavy and sustained pressure. Moreover, their monetary policies were not additionally burdened by the need to raise domestic interest rates significantly or for more than brief periods during the crises, to defend the exchange rate. In contrast, the market was considerably more skeptical of the sustainability of other ERM countries' currency pegs to the deutsche mark during the ERM crises. Speculative pressures led to the withdrawal of Italy and the United Kingdom from the ERM and devaluations by Spain, Ireland and Portugal. On some occasions, France was obliged to push its short-term interest rates to significant premiums over short-term German rates in order to sustain the exchange rate regime, despite economic fundamentals that suggested no overvaluation of the French franc vis-à-vis the deutsche mark. These experiences

suggest that in an environment of high capital mobility, pegged exchange rates among similar economies with strong linkages can be sustained, although this may require determined policy adjustments entailing significant but transitory economic costs.

More generally, although the ERM's adjustable peg system worked reasonably well to stabilize exchange rates among a growing number of European countries in the 1980s, it came under severe strain in the 1990s. The presence of some residual restrictions on international capital movements (removed completely only in 1990), as well as the willingness to make parity adjustments before disequilibria became too large, had contributed to the relatively smooth and successful functioning of the system in the earlier period. However, the system became vulnerable to asymmetric shocks due to increasing capital mobility and the hardening of exchange rate parities in response to the negotiation of the 1991 Maastricht Treaty on political and monetary union. In the event, the reunification of Germany's economy subjected the system to severe strains, culminating in the ERM crises of 1992–93. Where the market perceived that existing parities vis-à-vis the deutsche mark were overvalued or that cyclical conditions made the maintenance of high interest rates to defend exchange rate pegs questionable, exchange rates came under enormous market pressure. As a result, several ERM countries were forced to make significant adjustments to their central parities, or to abandon the ERM and float their currencies. Moreover, some other countries such as Finland and Sweden, which were not formally in the ERM, were forced to abandon their currencies' unilateral pegs. During the period from 1995, when Spain and Portugal realigned their ERM parities, until the advent of the euro in 1999, the ERM operated relatively smoothly, with wider fluctuation bands of plus or minus 15 percent. Progress in reducing macroeconomic imbalances and the imminent prospect of EMU also contributed to the ERM's smooth operation.

At least for the participating countries, the formation of EMU at the start of 1999 has removed the risk of exchange rate crises and vindicated efforts to achieve convergence, including through the pegging of exchange rates in the ERM. However, the lessons of the ERM crises of 1992–93 should not be lost. In an environment of high international capital mobility, when the market has some reason to question whether pegs can and will be sustained, pressures against the regime can become enormous and even very strong political commitments to sustain exchange rate pegs can be overwhelmed. Sustaining exchange rate pegs in an environment of high capital mobility requires the subordination of monetary policies to the exchange rate, combined with the credible capacity to tighten policy as may be re-

---

[16]The smaller industrial countries (with annual GDP below $20 billion), which include Iceland, Luxembourg, and San Marino, maintain rigid exchange rate pegs or use the national currency of a larger country or region.

quired to defend the peg. Moreover, the comparatively minor damage suffered by countries that adjusted or abandoned their pegs in the context of the ERM crises provides testimony that, by and large, their businesses and financial institutions prudently avoided substantial exposure to foreign exchange risk before the onset of the crises. Unfortunately, many businesses and financial institutions in several emerging market countries hit by more recent crises failed to exercise this kind of prudence.

Second, a number of medium-sized industrial countries have successfully maintained floating exchange rate regimes. After an earlier episode of floating its currency in the 1950s, Canada repegged to the U.S. dollar in 1962, and then moved back to a floating rate regime in 1970, before the general collapse of the Bretton Woods system. Notwithstanding the similarities of the two economies and the large weight of the United States in Canada's external trade, the Canadian economy is subject to different shocks (especially from commodity prices), and a floating exchange rate helps to absorb these differential shocks and the cyclical divergences between the two economies. Unlike most of the other smaller continental European countries, Switzerland has maintained a floating exchange rate regime that has not borne any apparent, substantial ill effects to the Swiss economy. Australia and New Zealand, which have diversified trade partners as well as significant dependence on commodity exports, also have chosen floating exchange rates and their economies appear to operate successfully under these regimes.

For medium-sized industrial countries with floating rate regimes, exchange rates generally are not subject to benign neglect. Unlike the United States, where the Federal Reserve typically pays little attention to the exchange rate in adjusting the federal funds rate, these countries regard the exchange rate as a key economic variable with a significant role in the conduct of monetary policy. For example, monetary policy decisions in Canada have long been guided by a "monetary conditions index" in which movements in the exchange rate as well as movements in short-term market interest rates are considered important in judging the monetary policy stance. Also, when the Canadian dollar's exchange rate moves sharply in a manner considered inappropriate, as occurred in August 1998, the Bank of Canada may adjust official interest rates to resist potentially destabilizing market dynamics. Switzerland, which has had persistently low inflation and generally sluggish economic growth for most of the last decade, has responded to occasional episodes of upward pressure on the exchange rate by monetary easing. The Bank of England, in determining the degree of monetary tightening needed to resist rising inflationary pressures in 1997 and early 1998, took account of a strong exchange rate as a factor likely to limit inflation, and, symmetrically, took account of a continued strong exchange rate in its subsequent decisions to ease monetary conditions as the projected inflation rate abated and the economy weakened.

Regardless of whether or not the floating exchange rates of medium-sized (as well as large) industrial countries are subject to benign neglect, exchange rates do move regularly and sometimes quite substantially in response to market forces. Intervention and adjustments of monetary policy may sometimes be used with a view to influencing exchange rates, but not with the intent or effect of creating de facto exchange rate pegs. This is very important because actual experience with fluctuations in market-determined exchange rates teaches and persuades private market participants, domestic and foreign, of the realities of foreign exchange risk. With such experience, institutions and practices evolve over time that enable the economic and financial system to adapt to the realities of a floating exchange rate regime.

Third, in the absence of an exchange rate peg, medium-sized industrial countries with floating exchange rate regimes have needed to establish an alternative nominal anchor for their monetary policies. During the 1970s, many of them were guided by the growth of monetary aggregates, for which some central banks announced formal targets. For Switzerland, the determined effort to contain inflationary pressures in the wake of the first oil shock in the mid-1970s was aided by a policy of monetary targeting. This firmly established the anti-inflation credentials of Swiss monetary policy and the independent credibility of the Swiss National Bank, even though monetary targets have since been abandoned. Despite some inflation slippage in the late 1980s, monetary policy credibility in Switzerland has never been seriously undermined. Other countries with floating exchange rate regimes have had less successful experiences with monetary targets and/or in achieving the fundamental objective of low inflation. For instance, in Australia, Canada, New Zealand, Sweden, and the United Kingdom, the establishment of monetary policy credibility has come more recently and has generally involved both the explicit adoption of an inflation target as the primary objective of monetary policy and the granting of operational independence to the central bank to pursue that objective. The lesson here is that, in the absence of an exchange rate peg as a nominal anchor, monetary policy generally needs a credible commitment to low inflation to provide an appropriate anchor, and this often can be facilitated by an inflation target and operational independence for the central bank.

In this connection, it should be emphasized that in the postwar era no industrial country has faced the problem of stabilizing its economy and financial system from a situation of very high inflation (annual inflation rates in the triple digits or higher). Rather, in recent years, industrial country experience lies in reducing inflation from moderate levels to very low levels. Hence, an assessment of the merits of alternative policy approaches for situations of very high inflation requires a careful look at the experience of developing countries.[17]

Finally, while essentially all industrial countries now have very liberal policies toward capital account transactions, many developing countries, in contrast, still maintain extensive restrictions on capital account transactions and often adjust these restrictions in light of pressures on their balance of payments. For these countries, the recent experience of industrial countries may be of comparatively limited relevance. Rather, one must look back to the period when many industrial countries maintained and

manipulated fairly extensive controls on international capital flows. In general, pegged exchange rate regimes were more sustainable and less subject to massive speculative attack during this period, regardless of the other problems capital controls may have generated.

However, the recent experience of industrial countries is increasingly relevant for emerging market countries that already are significantly integrated into modern, global capital markets, and for other developing and transition countries moving toward more liberal capital account regimes. With substantial openness to global capital markets, maintenance of exchange rate pegs requires the undiluted commitment of monetary policy and the capacity of the economy and the financial system to withstand the pressures generated by the interest rate adjustments that may occasionally be necessary to defend the peg. Even with firm policies and sound economic and financial structures, maintenance of the exchange rate peg can involve significant short-term costs in the face of substantial domestic or external shocks.

---

[17]See Appendix III for a discussion and references.

III   Exchange Rate Arrangements of Developing and Transition Countries

The developing and transition countries whose exchange arrangements are the subject of this section cover a very broad range of economic development—from the very poorest to the newly industrialized economies with per capita incomes at levels that categorize them, along with industrial countries, as "advanced economies." Correlated with the level of economic development, but not perfectly so, are both the degree of domestic financial sophistication and the extent of involvement with the global economic system, especially modern, global financial markets. The 30 or so countries that are most advanced in this last regard are commonly referred to as the "emerging markets."

In view of the wide economic and financial diversity among developing and transition countries, it is neither surprising nor untoward that there is considerable diversity in their exchange rate regimes—from very hard one-currency pegs to free floats and many variations in between.[18] Correspondingly, the purpose of this section is not to search for the one, ideal exchange rate regime that would fit all developing and transition countries. Rather, the aim is twofold: to elucidate the relationship between the circumstances of a country and the exchange regime that is most likely to suit its economic interests; and to discuss the factors required to make a chosen exchange rate regime function reasonably well in the circumstances of a particular country.

One characteristic shared by essentially all developing and transition countries and relevant for their exchange arrangements is that they must do the vast bulk of their international commerce and finance in terms of the monies of major industrial countries rather than in terms of their domestic monies. Thus, developing and transition countries with substantial involvement in international trade and finance have a deep interest in how the global economic and financial system operates. In particular, in deciding on their exchange arrangements, these countries must take as given the exchange rate fluctuations among the world's major currencies. Also, in contrast to the largest industrial countries, whose policies can influence conditions in the world economy and in global financial markets, developing and transition countries must take these conditions as given and adapt as best they can.

Adapting to expanding opportunities from deeper involvement in an increasingly integrated global economy and to changes in their own economic situations, developing and transition countries have been shifting their exchange rate regimes toward greater flexibility. At the same time, many of these countries have been moving toward current account convertibility and a somewhat less dramatic liberalization of capital account restrictions (Figure 3.1). The first part of this section considers key changes in the economic situations of developing and transition countries that have been associated with these policy developments. The second part of this section discusses the recent foreign exchange and financial crises that have affected many emerging market countries, and seeks to draw lessons from these experiences for exchange rate policy. Most importantly, countries that are tightening their links with modern, global financial markets are increasingly vulnerable to shifts in market sentiment, making the defense of pegged rates substantially more difficult. For those emerging market countries that still seek to maintain pegged exchange rates, as for the industrial countries discussed in the preceding section, the constraints on monetary policy and the need for sound economic and financial structures capable of withstanding pressures from defense of the peg are very demanding.

For many developing and transition countries, especially those with limited involvement in global financial markets, pegged exchange rates retain important advantages. Exchange rate pegs can provide a useful and credible nominal anchor for monetary policy and avoid many of the complexities and institutional requirements for establishing an alternative anchor (such as a functional and credible inflation

---

[18] For reviews of the literature on the choice of exchange rate regime, see among others Wickham (1985), Genberg (1989), Argy (1990), Edison and Melvin (1990), Aghevli, Khan, and Montiel (1991), Isard (1995), Obstfeld (1995a), Obstfeld and Rogoff (1995), IMF (1997, Chapter 4), Appendix I of Eichengreen, Masson, and others (1998), and Frankel (1999).

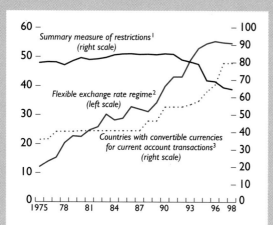

Figure 3.1. Developing Countries: Evolution of Exchange Rate Regimes and Exchange Restrictions
(In percent)

Source: IMF, *Annual Report on Exchange Arrangements and Exchange Restrictions.*

[1]Cross-country average of an index reflecting restrictions on capital account transactions, multiple exchange rates, and surrender of export proceeds. The index ranges from 0 when no restrictions are present to 100 when all restrictions are present. To reflect a change in methodology in 1996 for restrictions on capital account transactions, the 1996 and 1997 capital account restrictions indicators are rescaled so that the value in 1996 is the same as that in 1995. It is likely, however, that capital account liberalization took place between 1995 and 1996.

[2]In percent of total number of developing countries. Flexible exchange rate regimes include arrangements in which the exchange rate has limited flexibility with respect to another currency, is adjusted according to a set of indicators, follows a managed float, or is independently floating. The number for 1998 is preliminary.

[3]Percent of developing countries that have accepted Article VIII of the IMF's Articles of Agreement; countries are weighted by their 1990–95 share of aggregate exports of all developing countries.

target backed by an operationally independent central bank). Moreover, in the absence of sophisticated financial systems, many developing and transition countries lack the financial infrastructure to support a relatively deep and broad market for foreign exchange that could provide reasonable stability in the absence of official guidance concerning the exchange rate and policy support for that guidance.

The third part of this section considers the characteristics of countries for which some form of pegged exchange rate may be desirable and examines the relative virtues of alternative exchange rate regimes along the spectrum from hard pegs to free floats. This subsection also discusses the role of the exchange rate as a nominal anchor under various forms of pegged rate regimes, the need for an alternative nominal anchor under loosely managed or free

floats, and the use of intervention and controls by countries that do not practice benign neglect toward their exchange rates.

Exchange arrangements for countries that are in regional groups—notably the Association of Southeast Asian Nations (ASEAN) and the Southern Common Market (Mercosur) groups—with substantial intraregional trade and diversified economic linkages to the major industrial countries pose particular concerns. Alternative approaches to managing these concerns in the relatively near term are discussed in the fourth part of this section and longer-term options involving more ambitious efforts of regional cooperation are examined in Appendix V.

The section's conclusion summarizes the main implications for exchange regime choice by developing and transition countries in the present global economic environment.

Economic Environment Facing Developing and Transition Countries

Developing and transition countries face an economic environment undergoing significant changes that have important implications for their choice of exchange rate arrangements.

Increased Capital Mobility

Gross capital flows to developing countries have risen considerably as a share of their GDP since the early 1980s (Figure 3.2). This trend reflects greater capital account liberalization and capital market integration, especially of emerging market economies.[19] Higher gross flows have created the potential for large and sudden reversals in net flows, particularly in the case of private flows (excluding foreign direct investment). Net private flows to developing countries, after hovering around ½ percent of GDP throughout the 1970s and 1980s, rose sharply to 3 percent of GDP in the mid-1990s, only to drop back to 1½ percent of GDP in 1998. Similar developments are also evident in the case of outstanding bank claims, which fell abruptly in Asia, Latin America, and Eastern Europe in the context of the recent emerging market crises (Figure 3.3), discussed in the next subsection.[20] As is well known, capital flow reversals have been associated with currency crises and

---

[19] Since the concept of transition countries has only become relevant during the last decade or so, Figures 3.1 through 3.8 concentrate on developing countries.

[20] Developments in capital flows are analyzed in greater detail in Mussa, Swoboda, Zettelmeyer, and Jeanne (1999).

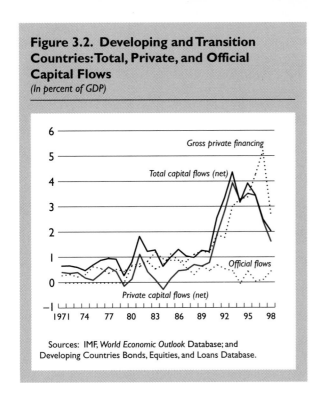

Figure 3.2. Developing and Transition Countries: Total, Private, and Official Capital Flows
(In percent of GDP)

Sources: IMF, *World Economic Outlook* Database; and Developing Countries Bonds, Equities, and Loans Database.

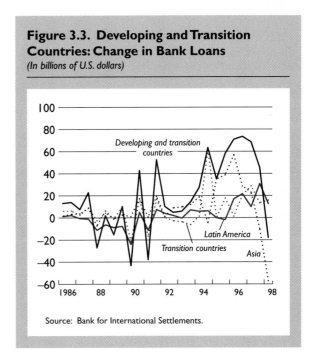

Figure 3.3. Developing and Transition Countries: Change in Bank Loans
(In billions of U.S. dollars)

Source: Bank for International Settlements.

large real economic costs. However, this phenomenon of the boom/bust cycle in private capital flows and its attendant costs are relevant primarily for the emerging market economies that have important involvement in modern global financial markets. It has not directly affected the wide range of developing countries with little or no such involvement.

Exposure to Exchange Rate Risk

As previously noted, residents of developing and transition countries generally find it difficult to borrow abroad in their own currencies, and nonresidents are generally reluctant to take net long positions in those currencies. In net terms, the foreign currency liabilities of residents of developing and transition countries usually exceed their assets in foreign currencies, implying that they are exposed to exchange rate risk on their balance sheets as well as through trade. Issues of both sovereign and corporate bonds on international markets are overwhelmingly in foreign currencies, even in the case of an advanced economy such as Korea, or a country whose exchange rate is strongly pegged to the U.S. dollar, such as Argentina.[21] Part of this exchange rate risk can be hedged, although only (in the aggregate for a given

developing country) to the limited extent that nonresidents are willing to hold local currency exposure.[22] Moreover, few of these countries have organized markets for currency futures and options, and those markets located in industrial countries deal mainly in industrial country currencies (IMF, 1995a, Appendix Table 4).[23] Also, while forward foreign exchange contracts are allowed in many emerging markets (IMF, 1995b, p. 22), there is no indication of significant net capacity to shift foreign exchange risks abroad at a reasonable price.

Portfolio Diversification

A consequence of globalization has been a greater internationalization of balance sheets, with the private and public sectors of emerging market countries holding and issuing an increasing quantity and variety of foreign currency assets and liabilities. For instance, 28 percent of the international bonds issued by emerging market countries in 1996–98 were denominated in a currency other than the U.S. dollar, with the recent launch of the euro significantly raising the share of the nondollar sector to 33 percent

---

[21] This might not necessarily imply exposure to exchange rate risk for those corporations whose receipts are largely in foreign currency.

[22] Hedging can take many forms, including nonresidents holding local-currency-denominated equities. For example, in 1996, the share of total market capitalization held by nonresidents in the stock markets of Argentina, Korea, Mexico, Thailand, and the Philippines ranged from 15–40 percent (World Bank, 1997, p. 306).

[23] However, currency futures are available in the United States for the Brazilian real, the Mexican peso, and the Russian ruble.

during the first half of 1999.[24] However, discussions with market participants (by staff in the IMF's capital markets group) reveal that the market of dedicated investors in the liabilities of emerging market countries is, at best, very limited.

Increased Openness to International Trade

The developing economies' degree of openness to international trade has increased over the past few decades. The average share of external trade (measured by exports plus imports, divided by two) in GDP for all developing countries rose from about 30 percent in the late 1960s to about 40 percent in the late 1990s (Figure 3.4). This trend has been more marked in the case of the east Asian countries—mirroring their export-led growth.[25] With imports and exports representing a larger share of developing countries' GDP, given changes in the exchange rate have a greater impact on output and prices.

Shift of Exports Toward Manufactures

At the same time, the composition of developing countries' trade by type of product has changed considerably, with a move away from commodity exports and toward manufactured exports (Figure 3.5), especially for emerging market economies. This shift in composition has made developing countries' terms of trade more stable, but it has also made those countries with growing manufactured exports more sensitive to exchange rate fluctuations. Prices of most commodities are set in global markets, and supply and demand for individual exporters are largely independent of the exchange rate. In contrast, supply and demand for exports of manufactured products show significant sensitivity to exchange rates (Eichengreen, Masson, and others, 1998, p. 37).

Trade Diversification

Consistent with the trend toward globalization, many developing—and especially emerging market—economies now trade with a wide range of partner countries. With the notable exception of Mexico, which conducts four-fifths of its trade with the United States, a typical medium-sized developing country's share of trade with a single currency area is below one-half in the case of countries in Africa, the Middle East, and Europe, and below one-third in the case of countries in Asia and Latin

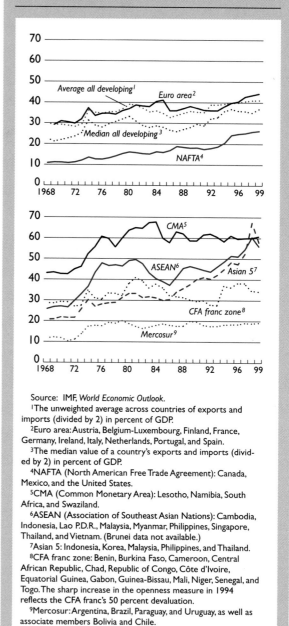

Figure 3.4. Advanced and Developing Countries: Measures of Openness of Economies

Source: IMF, *World Economic Outlook*.
[1]The unweighted average across countries of exports and imports (divided by 2) in percent of GDP.
[2]Euro area: Austria, Belgium-Luxembourg, Finland, France, Germany, Ireland, Italy, Netherlands, Portugal, and Spain.
[3]The median value of a country's exports and imports (divided by 2) in percent of GDP.
[4]NAFTA (North American Free Trade Agreement): Canada, Mexico, and the United States.
[5]CMA (Common Monetary Area): Lesotho, Namibia, South Africa, and Swaziland.
[6]ASEAN (Association of Southeast Asian Nations): Cambodia, Indonesia, Lao P.D.R., Malaysia, Myanmar, Philippines, Singapore, Thailand, and Vietnam. (Brunei data not available.)
[7]Asian 5: Indonesia, Korea, Malaysia, Philippines, and Thailand.
[8]CFA franc zone: Benin, Burkina Faso, Cameroon, Central African Republic, Chad, Republic of Congo, Côte d'Ivoire, Equatorial Guinea, Gabon, Guinea-Bissau, Mali, Niger, Senegal, and Togo. The sharp increase in the openness measure in 1994 reflects the CFA franc's 50 percent devaluation.
[9]Mercosur: Argentina, Brazil, Paraguay, and Uruguay, as well as associate members Bolivia and Chile.

America.[26] There are usually large trade shares with at least two of the major currency areas (the United States, the euro area, and Japan), implying

---

[24] Source: Capital Data Ltd.
[25] See Ito and others (1996).

[26] The geographical trade patterns for selected developing and transition countries are provided in Table 3.1.

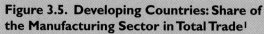

Figure 3.5. Developing Countries: Share of the Manufacturing Sector in Total Trade[1]

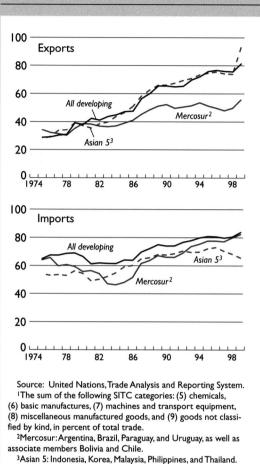

Source: United Nations, Trade Analysis and Reporting System.
[1]The sum of the following SITC categories: (5) chemicals, (6) basic manufactures, (7) machines and transport equipment, (8) miscellaneous manufactured goods, and (9) goods not classified by kind, in percent of total trade.
[2]Mercosur: Argentina, Brazil, Paraguay, and Uruguay, as well as associate members Bolivia and Chile.
[3]Asian 5: Indonesia, Korea, Malaysia, Philippines, and Thailand.

that developing countries with single-currency pegs remain significantly exposed to the wide fluctuations among major currencies documented in Section II.

Greater Intraregional Trade

The importance of intraregional trade for developing countries, though still moderate compared with their trade with industrial countries, is increasing, especially for key regional groups of emerging market economies. Table 3.2 illustrates this by considering several regions, including Mercosur, five east Asian countries most affected by the recent emerging market crises, ASEAN, the countries in Central and Eastern Europe that initiated accession negotiations with the European Union in March 1998, and the CFA franc zone. For comparison purposes, data on the euro area and the North American Free Trade

Agreement countries (NAFTA) are also presented. As shown in Tables 3.2 and 3.3, intraregional trade in each of these regions has increased substantially during the last decade.[27] The growing importance of intraregional trade for key developing countries has increased the magnitude of the real effects of the fluctuations in the bilateral exchange rates between neighbor (or near-neighbor) developing countries.[28]

Reduced Inflation

An important development in recent years has been the fall in inflation in most developing countries. The median inflation rate fell to about 5 percent in the late 1990s from the 10 percent or more prevailing between the early 1970s and the early 1990s (Figure 3.6).[29] While the widespread decline of inflation in developing and transition countries has benefited from positive supply shocks (in particular lower petroleum prices) and the anti-inflationary environment in industrial countries, it also reveals the broad acceptance now among the public of these countries that the key objective of monetary policy should be to deliver low inflation, that prudent macroeconomic policies are beneficial, and, correspondingly, that fiscal policy should not rely on the inflation tax.

Lessons from Recent Emerging Market Crises

Recent crises involving emerging market economies, from the "tequila crisis"[30] of 1995 through the Asian/Russian/Brazilian crises of 1997–98, carry important lessons for exchange regimes of developing and transition countries. Indeed, these experiences have led qualified observers, such as Eichengreen and others (1999), to conclude that pegged exchange rate regimes are inherently crisis-prone for emerging market economies and that these countries should be encouraged, in their own interest and for the broader interests of the international community, to adopt floating rate regimes. This, together with a move by a number of other

---

[27] Data for Central East European countries (CEEC) negotiating EU accession cover too short a period to draw any firm conclusions and, in any case, this set of countries has no particular significance as a regional trading group. The strength of their trade linkages with the EU is a more important consideration for the purposes of this analysis.
[28] Table 3.3 shows the shares of regional trade as a percentage of total regional GDP (for the same groups considered in Table 3.2).
[29] The recent decline in inflation worldwide is analyzed in the October 1996 *World Economic Outlook* (IMF, 1996, Chapter 6).
[30] The financial crisis that followed the December 1994 devaluation of the Mexican peso.

Table 3.1. Selected Developing and Transition Countries: Trade Shares and Openness

	1998 Trade Share with				1998 Proportion of Trade in GDP[1]
	United States	Germany	Japan	Euro Area	
Latin America					
Argentina	14.2	4.3	3.7	20.0	10.2
Brazil	21.7	7.7	5.0	24.8	8.2
Chile	18.8	4.4	8.8	17.9	27.1
Colombia	35.5	5.4	4.9	17.5	17.5
Costa Rica	51.6	3.7	2.5	14.2	47.7
Ecuador	33.7	4.2	6.2	15.1	29.4
Mexico	77.8	2.4	2.6	5.9	25.0
Paraguay	16.3	1.4	3.0	10.7	26.0
Peru	29.4	4.1	4.7	15.7	15.7
Uruguay	11.4	3.5	1.9	16.0	21.5
Venezuela	43.0	2.7	2.5	10.8	20.3
Asia					
China, Mainland	17.5	4.3	15.0	11.4	19.6
China, Hong Kong	15.2	3.0	9.0	8.8	124.7
India	14.9	5.8	5.8	19.8	12.4
Indonesia	12.8	4.6	17.3	12.7	71.4
Korea	16.9	2.8	12.4	8.4	44.1
Malaysia	18.1	3.2	12.9	9.0	115.5
Pakistan	15.2	5.2	6.2	16.9	14.6
Philippines	24.8	3.0	16.5	8.9	56.4
Singapore	18.2	2.3	10.8	10.1	143.6
Thailand	17.1	3.5	17.2	12.0	49.5
Africa					
Central African Republic	1.5	0.9	1.3	44.5	20.6
Ethiopia	6.8	10.6	7.8	29.7	21.6
Gabon	39.1	1.8	2.4	34.3	47.0
Ghana	7.2	5.7	3.0	34.0	29.9
Guinea	11.8	2.7	1.6	46.4	21.5
Kenya	5.4	5.1	4.3	17.9	30.5
Mauritius	7.5	4.9	2.9	30.0	62.4
Morocco	5.1	6.4	2.0	57.1	29.7
Nigeria	25.8	5.1	1.7	29.3	18.9
South Africa	10.5	9.3	6.1	25.6	29.0
Zambia	2.9	1.8	6.5	11.1	33.8
Zimbabwe	4.1	3.9	4.5	13.6	47.3
Middle East and Europe					
Egypt	15.7	9.2	4.9	34.2	21.8
Iran	0.0	10.6	7.5	35.0	16.4
Israel	28.9	6.6	3.6	31.3	39.9
Jordan	7.2	6.5	4.9	21.0	63.0
Kuwait	24.5	5.7	26.5	20.7	51.3
Saudi Arabia	19.7	3.5	12.1	16.7	34.1
Turkey	8.1	18.0	2.6	42.1	27.2
Central and Eastern Europe					
Czech Republic	2.1	35.0	0.6	54.9	60.9
Estonia	2.9	8.6	0.7	43.3	82.0
Hungary	4.0	34.3	1.8	65.5	60.8
Latvia	4.7	15.6	0.3	35.6	56.2
Lithuania	2.9	16.2	1.3	32.7	62.3
Poland	2.3	31.4	0.6	59.2	27.5
Romania	3.9	19.2	0.5	51.7	26.6
Russia	7.8	9.8	2.6	28.1	28.6
Slovak Republic	1.1	27.5	0.2	47.6	58.7
Slovenia	2.9	24.3	1.0	63.4	56.1
Ukraine	2.0	5.2	0.3	12.5	42.9

Sources: IMF, *World Economic Outlook* database, and *Direction of Trade Statistics.*
[1]The average of exports and imports in percent of GDP.

Table 3.2. Regional Trade Patterns, 1980–98 (selected years)
(In percent of total regional trade)

	1980 Exports	1980 Imports	1985 Exports	1985 Imports	1990 Exports	1990 Imports	1995 Exports	1995 Imports	1998 Exports	1998 Imports
Mercosur[1]										
Within Mercosur	15.8	11.3	8.2	13.8	11.6	17.5	22.6	20.2	26.8	22.7
With the United States	14.7	20.3	22.8	19.1	20.4	19.3	15.0	20.6	15.1	21.6
With euro area	27.4	17.8	24.4	15.9	28.8	20.1	21.3	22.3	21.3	22.0
With other industrial countries	13.3	14.7	12.1	12.8	14.6	15.4	14.3	13.7	10.6	13.3
With other developing countries	27.1	35.2	30.0	36.5	23.2	26.6	26.0	22.1	25.0	19.5
Asian 5[2]										
Within Asian 5	4.9	6.0	6.4	7.8	6.7	6.6	8.4	8.1	10.2	12.5
With Japan	29.9	25.1	24.7	23.8	22.2	26.1	15.9	25.8	11.6	17.8
With the United States	20.8	18.3	26.1	18.4	23.9	18.2	19.5	17.3	20.2	14.4
With euro area	11.8	8.7	8.6	9.7	11.8	11.3	10.4	11.6	10.7	8.6
With other industrial countries	5.8	9.7	7.9	10.9	8.3	10.6	6.6	9.4	8.1	7.4
With other developing countries	25.6	31.0	24.7	26.2	25.0	24.1	36.9	26.1	36.5	36.6
ASEAN[3]										
Within ASEAN	17.4	14.6	18.6	17.2	19.0	15.2	24.6	18.0	22.1	24.1
With Japan	29.6	22.3	25.1	20.5	18.9	23.1	14.2	23.8	11.1	16.9
With the United States	16.3	15.3	19.5	15.2	19.4	14.4	18.6	13.8	20.6	13.8
With euro area	10.4	9.6	8.4	10.0	11.7	11.2	10.8	11.1	11.9	8.9
With other industrial countries	6.1	10.3	6.2	9.7	7.6	9.8	6.9	8.1	8.6	6.7
With other developing countries	20.2	28.6	21.5	26.7	23.1	25.2	24.3	24.3	25.2	28.5
CFA franc zone[4]										
Within CFA franc zone	6.6	6.1	6.8	6.7	8.1	9.3	6.7	6.9	8.5	8.5
With euro area	56.7	57.6	53.2	53.9	50.9	52.0	46.1	45.8	40.7	45.6
With other industrial countries	18.1	14.7	22.8	18.1	20.9	14.3	22.5	14.7	21.1	12.5
With other developing countries	18.9	21.2	14.0	18.7	18.0	21.1	21.7	29.2	26.2	29.6
CEEC 5[5]										
Within CEEC 5	...	...	...	...	...	...	5.9	4.7	6.5	4.7
With euro area	...	...	...	...	...	...	56.7	54.5	57.4	60.4
With other industrial countries	...	...	...	...	...	...	11.9	16.3	14.2	12.9
With other developing countries	...	...	...	...	...	...	23.7	23.9	21.7	21.6
Euro area[6]										
Within euro area	50.6	44.2	47.1	46.1	54.1	52.8	51.2	50.7	48.7	48.5
With Japan	0.9	2.3	1.2	3.1	2.0	4.1	2.0	3.8	1.6	3.8
With the United States	4.7	7.8	8.9	7.2	6.1	6.7	5.9	6.8	7.6	7.8
With other industrial countries	18.5	15.6	20.2	17.2	19.5	16.7	18.3	16.8	18.9	16.6
With other developing countries	23.5	29.7	21.0	25.8	17.2	19.1	21.3	21.0	22.0	22.4
NAFTA[7]										
Within NAFTA	33.6	32.8	43.9	34.4	41.4	33.9	46.2	38.4	51.0	40.4
With Japan	8.3	10.6	8.8	16.9	10.5	15.2	8.6	13.7	6.4	10.9
With euro area	17.4	10.3	13.5	13.7	15.6	13.2	11.7	11.6	11.3	12.4
With other industrial countries	10.1	7.9	8.4	7.9	9.4	7.8	7.2	6.2	7.6	6.2
With other developing countries	28.8	37.0	23.9	26.4	23.0	29.1	26.1	29.8	23.6	29.7

Source: IMF, *Direction of Trade Statistics.*

[1]Mercosur: Argentina, Brazil, Paraguay, Uruguay, and associate members Bolivia and Chile.

[2] Asian 5: Indonesia, Korea, Malaysia, Philippines, and Thailand.

[3] ASEAN (Association of Southeast Asian Nations): Cambodia, Indonesia, Laos, Malaysia, Myanmar, Philippines, Singapore, Thailand, and Vietnam (Brunei data are not available).

[4]CFA franc zone: Benin, Burkina Faso, Cameroon, Central African Republic, Chad, Republic of Congo, Côte d'Ivoire, Equatorial Guinea, Gabon, Guinea-Bissau, Mali, Niger, Senegal, and Togo.

[5]CEEC 5: Czech Republic, Estonia, Hungary, Poland, and Slovenia - the countries that initiated accession negotiations with the European Union in March 1998, a group chosen purely for illustration purposes.

[6]Euro area: Austria, Belgium, Finland, France, Germany, Ireland, Italy, Luxembourg, Netherlands, Portugal, and Spain.

[7]NAFTA (North American Free Trade Association): Canada, Mexico, and the United States.

Table 3.3. Regional Trade Patterns, 1980–98 (selected years)
(In percent of total regional GDP)

	1980		1985		1990		1995		1998	
	Exports	Imports	Exports	Imports	Exports	Imports	Exports	Imports	Exports	Imports
Mercosur[1]										
Within Mercosur	1.1	1.1	1.0	1.0	1.0	1.1	1.8	1.8	2.1	2.3
With the United States	1.1	1.9	2.8	1.4	1.7	1.2	1.2	1.8	1.2	2.2
With euro area	2.0	1.7	3.0	1.2	2.4	1.2	1.7	2.0	1.7	2.3
With other industrial countries	1.0	1.4	1.5	1.0	1.2	0.9	1.2	1.2	0.9	1.4
With other developing countries	2.0	3.3	3.7	2.7	2.0	1.6	2.1	2.0	2.0	2.0
Asian 5[2]										
Within Asian 5	1.3	1.5	1.7	1.9	1.9	2.0	2.7	2.9	5.7	5.9
With Japan	8.1	6.4	6.5	5.7	6.2	8.1	5.1	9.3	6.4	8.4
With the United States	5.6	4.7	6.9	4.4	6.7	5.7	6.3	6.2	11.3	6.8
With euro area	3.2	2.2	2.3	2.3	3.3	3.5	3.3	4.2	6.0	4.0
With other industrial countries	1.6	2.5	2.1	2.6	2.3	3.3	2.1	3.4	4.5	3.5
With other developing countries	6.9	7.9	6.5	6.2	7.0	7.5	11.9	9.4	20.3	17.3
ASEAN[3]										
Within ASEAN	5.6	4.2	5.8	4.9	7.6	6.9	10.6	8.8	11.7	11.8
With Japan	9.5	6.5	7.8	5.8	7.6	10.5	6.2	11.7	5.9	8.3
With the United States	5.2	4.4	6.0	4.3	7.8	6.6	8.1	6.8	10.9	6.8
With euro area	3.4	2.8	2.6	2.8	4.7	5.1	4.7	5.5	6.3	4.3
With other industrial countries	2.0	3.0	1.9	2.7	3.0	4.5	3.0	4.0	4.5	3.3
With other developing countries	6.5	8.3	6.6	7.6	9.3	11.5	10.5	11.9	13.4	14.0
CFA franc zone[4]										
Within CFA franc zone	1.8	1.5	2.0	1.6	1.8	1.8	1.8	1.9	2.6	2.8
With euro area	15.0	14.5	15.8	13.0	11.3	10.1	12.2	12.5	12.5	15.0
With other industrial countries	4.8	3.7	6.8	4.4	4.6	2.8	6.0	4.0	6.5	4.1
With other developing countries	5.0	5.3	4.2	4.5	4.0	4.1	5.7	8.0	8.1	9.8
CEEC 5[5]										
Within CEEC 5	...	...	...	...	...	...	1.6	1.6	2.0	2.2
With euro area	...	...	...	...	...	...	15.1	18.3	17.7	27.9
With other industrial countries	...	...	...	...	...	...	3.2	5.5	4.4	6.0
With other developing countries	...	...	...	...	...	...	6.3	8.0	6.7	10.0
Euro area[6]										
Within euro area	11.4	11.3	12.5	12.3	12.6	12.4	12.4	11.4	12.8	12.0
With Japan	0.2	0.6	0.3	0.8	0.5	1.0	0.5	0.9	0.4	1.0
With the United States	1.1	2.0	2.4	1.9	1.4	1.6	1.4	1.5	2.0	2.0
With other industrial countries	4.2	4.0	5.3	4.6	4.5	3.9	4.4	3.8	5.0	4.2
With other developing countries	5.3	7.6	5.6	6.9	4.0	4.5	5.2	4.7	5.8	5.6
NAFTA[7]										
Within NAFTA	3.1	3.5	3.0	3.4	3.4	3.5	4.8	4.9	5.3	5.4
With Japan	0.8	1.1	0.6	1.7	0.9	1.6	0.9	1.7	0.7	1.5
With euro area	1.6	1.1	0.9	1.3	1.3	1.4	1.2	1.5	1.2	1.7
With other industrial countries	0.9	0.8	0.6	0.8	0.8	0.8	0.8	0.8	0.8	0.8
With other developing countries	2.7	3.9	1.7	2.6	1.9	3.0	2.7	3.8	2.5	4.0

Sources: IMF, *Direction of Trade Statistics*, and *World Economic Outlook*.

[1]Mercosur: Argentina, Brazil, Paraguay, Uruguay, and associate members Bolivia and Chile.

[2]Asian 5: Indonesia, Korea, Malaysia, Philippines, and Thailand.

[3]ASEAN (Association of Southeast Asian Nations): Cambodia, Indonesia, Laos, Malaysia, Myanmar, Philippines, Singapore, Thailand, and Vietnam (Brunei data are not available).

[4]CFA franc zone: Benin, Burkina Faso, Cameroon, Central African Republic, Chad, Republic of Congo, Côte d'Ivoire, Equatorial Guinea, Gabon, Guinea-Bissau, Mali, Niger, Senegal, and Togo.

[5]CEEC 5: Czech Republic, Estonia, Hungary, Poland, and Slovenia—the countries that initiated accession negotiations with the European Union in March 1998, a group chosen purely for illustration purposes.

[6]Euro area: Austria, Belgium, Finland, France, Germany, Ireland, Italy, Luxembourg, Netherlands, Portugal, and Spain.

[7]NAFTA (North American Free Trade Association): Canada, Mexico, and the United States.

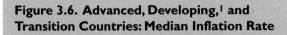

Figure 3.6. Advanced, Developing,[1] and Transition Countries: Median Inflation Rate

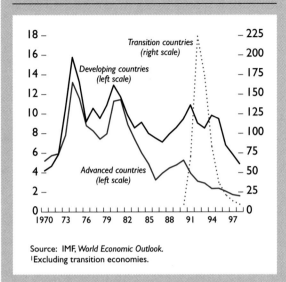

Source: IMF, *World Economic Outlook.*
[1]Excluding transition economies.

countries toward hard pegs, suggests a "hollowing of the middle" of the spectrum of exchange rate regimes from very hard pegs to pure floats.[31]

In considering this conclusion, it is important to stress a critical caveat: while recent crises have directly and adversely affected many emerging market economies with important links to modern global financial markets, these crises have only indirectly affected (through movements in world commodity prices and trade flows) the majority of developing and transition countries. Accordingly, lessons for exchange rate regimes from these crises relate primarily to emerging market countries (and to countries that may soon join this group) and not necessarily more broadly.

Taking account of this essential caveat, it must be recognized that for those emerging market countries that were most severely affected by recent crises, their exchange rate regimes were clearly important factors in their vulnerability.[32] The most severely af-

---

[31] An early version of the "hollowing of the middle" thesis, based on the argument that intermediate exchange rate regimes of the target zone and adjustable peg variety are not credible or inconsistent with proposed macroeconomic policies, especially under increasing capital mobility, can be found in Swoboda (1986).

[32]Argentina and Mexico were the most severely affected countries in the tequila crisis; Indonesia, Korea, Malaysia, Thailand, and (to a lesser extent) Hong Kong SAR were most severely affected in the Asian crisis; Russia was most severely affected in the Russian crisis; and Brazil and Argentina were most severely affected in the Brazilian crisis. Colombia, Ecuador, and Venezuela are presently feeling primarily the effects of their own difficulties rather than the spillovers from the broader crises affecting emerging markets.

fected countries all had de jure or de facto exchange rate pegs or otherwise substantially limited the movement of their exchange rates. In contrast, emerging market economies that maintained greater flexibility in their exchange rate regimes generally fared much better. For example, Chile, Mexico, Peru, South Africa, and Turkey all seem to have benefited from the flexibility of their exchange rates during the recent international financial crisis.

When drawing conclusions from these comparisons, however, it also should be noted that it is precisely in circumstances like those in recent crises that flexible exchange rate regimes (in place and operating before the crisis and not adopted during the crisis) should be expected to perform better. A flexible exchange rate regime allows large adverse shocks to be more easily deflected or absorbed than a pegged or quasi-pegged exchange rate regime, and avoids the large costs that often accompany a breakdown of the exchange rate regime (in comparison with the adjustment of an already flexible exchange rate).

A reasoned judgment on the desirable exchange rate regime thus needs to be based not only on how it performs in a crisis, but how it performs on average over time. For instance, Argentina, with its currency board, has had strong growth in the 1990s, despite the negative effects of the tequila and Russian crises. That said, it must be emphasized that the costs of recent crises to the most affected countries have been very large, and especially so for those countries whose pegged or quasi–pegged exchange regimes broke down in the throes of crisis. There is an undeniable lesson here about the difficulties and dangers of running pegged or quasi–pegged exchange rate regimes for emerging market economies with substantial involvement in global capital markets, as evidenced by the fact that only the emerging market countries with the hardest pegs were able to maintain their exchange rates.

Of course, important factors other than the relative fixity of their exchange rate regimes contributed significantly to the problems of those countries most affected by recent emerging market crises. Russia's most important problem was, and is, the chronic incapacity of the central government to meet its fiscal responsibilities and the broader problems of the general culture of nonpayment and noncompliance with ordinary commercial practices and obligations. Brazil, too, has had a serious fiscal problem. For Korea, the principal problem was not a seriously overvalued exchange rate, but rather a weak financial system and many weak and overleveraged corporations. For Thailand and Malaysia and (to a lesser extent) Indonesia, overvaluation of the exchange rate was more of an issue, but weaknesses in the financial sector and in the financial position of nonfinancial businesses were also critical. In general, it was not the exchange rate regime alone that was the fundamental source of precrisis vulnerability and of subsequent substantial damage. And changing the exchange rate regime will not automatically correct (although, as discussed below, it may help ameliorate) these other critical problems.

Moreover, with sounder, better managed, and better supervised financial systems, and with stronger incentives for lower leverage and lower foreign-exchange exposure of domestic businesses and households, governments would be better able to raise domestic interest rates when needed to defend the exchange rate, and would be more credible in pursuing such a policy. If exposure to foreign-currency-denominated debt were more limited,[33] exchange rate adjustments could be undertaken with less damage and less reason for delay. Improvements in these key areas, which are desirable in their own right, would tend to make pegged exchange rate regimes less dangerous and more tenable for countries with significant involvement in modern global financial markets. Indeed, for countries with important links to global financial markets, successful operation of pegged exchange rates requires both the dedication of monetary policy to the exchange rate objective and sufficient strength in the country's economic and financial system to withstand the pressures from sharp interest rate adjustments that may occasionally be needed to defend the peg.

Notwithstanding the potential for improvement in these other areas, however, it is essential to recognize that the countries most adversely affected by recent crises experienced an intrinsic perversity in the interactions between their exchange rate regimes and other problems in their economies, especially weaknesses in their financial sectors. When the exchange rate is pegged or tightly managed and it is believed that this will continue, there is often little perceived risk for domestic firms or financial institutions to borrow in foreign currency. If domestic-currency interest rates rise above foreign-currency rates (because of efforts to contain domestic overheating by tighter monetary policy together with sterilized intervention to resist exchange rate appreciation), then there is a positive incentive to borrow foreign currency. As international credits are generally most cheaply and easily available for short maturities, foreign-currency borrowing tends to be short term.

If, because of adverse domestic or international developments, market sentiment turns and the ex-

change rate comes under downward pressure, the national authorities are understandably reluctant to resist by raising domestic interest rates, as this will further undermine already weak banks and businesses. Adjustment of the exchange rate is also resisted—through sterilized official intervention—because a substantial depreciation would raise the burdens of foreign-currency-denominated debts.[34] Once it becomes clear that the authorities are caught in a situation where they want to defend the exchange rate, but dare not raise domestic interest rates (credibly and substantially), and are running short of reserves, then speculative pressures against the exchange rate become overwhelming. If the peg is broken, depreciation is likely to be substantial as private agents rush to cover their remaining foreign exchange exposures and as foreign and domestic capital attempts to flee the developing crisis. The authorities, with limited remaining reserves, are in a poor position to help stabilize the rate, and the market that is not used to operating without official support tends to become illiquid and move erratically. Downward pressures build as recognition of the adverse consequences of financial disruption associated with massive depreciation become mutually reinforcing. Thus, pegged or quasi-pegged exchange rates (or heavily managed floats) do tend to contribute to other problems that make these regimes prone to damaging financial crises. The likelihood of prolonged speculative attack and, indeed, of a downturn in sentiment is reduced to the extent that the credibility of the peg is high; this is most obvious in the case of a currency board.

A genuine floating exchange rate, by contrast, allows greater flexibility for monetary policy at times of exchange rate pressures and economic difficulty. Also, provided that the exchange rate really does move up and down in response to market forces, businesses and financial institutions are forced to recognize the risks inherent in foreign-currency borrowing and other exposures to foreign exchange risk. Floating does not preclude the use of official intervention and adjustments of monetary policy to influence the exchange rate. However, efforts to tightly manage the exchange rate primarily through (sterilized) official intervention tend to recreate the risks and problems of a pegged exchange rate. If

---

[33] Unfortunately, pegged rates tend to encourage foreign currency borrowing by domestic banks and nonfinancial firms.

[34] Beyond normal intervention, the authorities may resort to the forward market (Thailand in 1997) or futures market (Brazil, 1997–98), or they may exchange domestic-currency debt for foreign-currency linked debt (Mexico, 1994; and Brazil, 1997–98), or they may loan official reserves to domestic institutions experiencing financing difficulties (Korea, 1997). These strategies may help to forestall a crisis, but if the crisis breaks they can also make it much more damaging.

the exchange rate is managed, interest rates should be a primary tool so that private sector behavior will be appropriately attuned to situations where aggressive interest rate adjustments may occasionally be required to support the exchange rate objective. For countries substantially involved in modern global financial markets, policy regimes that seek to provide a high degree of stability of both exchange rates and interest rates, and that induce private risk taking on the presumption that both are simultaneously possible, are an invitation to trouble.

Exchange Regime Choice: Emerging Markets and Beyond

The preceding discussion strongly suggests that for emerging market countries with substantial involvement in modern global financial markets, floating exchange rate regimes should be an increasingly relevant, albeit not universal, choice. Looking beyond the emerging market economies to the large number of developing and transition countries that do not (yet) have close links with modern, global financial markets, the rigors of maintaining a pegged exchange rate regime are less demanding. For such countries, and especially those lacking a well-developed financial infrastructure including sophisticated financial institutions and broad and deep markets for foreign exchange, pegs can provide a simple and credible anchor for monetary policy. While the precise requirements for a successful float are not the subject of this paper, it can safely be said that many developing and transition economies do not satisfy them. Indeed, while an increasing number of them (including many emerging market economies) officially describe their exchange rate regimes as "managed floating" or "independent floating" (see Figure 3.1 and Table A2.1 in Appendix II), the fact is that most of them maintain some form of de jure or de facto exchange rate peg or otherwise narrowly limit fluctuations of the exchange rate.[35] The economic criteria usually thought to influence the appropriateness of adopting a fixed, as opposed to a flexible, exchange rate regime provide at least a partial explanation of this phenomenon.

Specifically, the following conditions are likely to influence whether some form of pegged exchange rate regime is judged to be appropriate: [36]

- The degree of involvement with international capital markets is low;
- The share of trade with the country to which it is pegged is high;
- The shocks it faces are similar to those facing the country to which it pegs;
- It is willing to give up monetary independence for its partner's monetary credibility;
- Its economy and financial system already extensively rely on its partner's currency;
- Because of high inherited inflation, exchange-rate-based stabilization is attractive;
- Its fiscal policy is flexible and sustainable;
- Its labor markets are flexible;
- It has high international reserves.

Countries with Pegged Exchange Rate Regimes

Applying these criteria, one group of countries for which pegged exchange rates would seem to remain sensible are small economies with a dominant trading partner that maintains a reasonably stable monetary policy. For such countries, there is generally little point in incurring the costs of attempting to run an independent monetary policy. As shown in Appendix II, IMF members with an annual GDP of less than $5 billion overwhelmingly have pegged exchange rate regimes. For most of these countries, it is clear not only that they should peg; the currencies to which they should peg are also clear. Small Caribbean island economies, some small central American countries, and some Pacific island economies peg to the U.S. dollar. The CFA franc zone countries peg to the French franc (and, since 1999, to the euro). Lesotho, Namibia, and Swaziland peg to the South African rand. Bhutan and Nepal (which has an annual GDP slightly above $5 billion)

---

[35] The example of the Malaysian currency, the ringgit, illustrates the difficulties with regard to the difference between official and practical definitions of exchange rate regime. The ringgit was in practice pegged quite closely to the U.S. dollar prior to the Thai crisis, for example fluctuating within a range of RM2.47–2.52:$1 in the first half of 1997. Nevertheless, the authorities characterized that regime as a managed float.

[36] Since available empirical studies on the effects of alternative regimes on economic performance (e.g., Ghosh and others, 1995; IMF, 1997; Hausmann and others, 1999) do not control for these conditions, they are not very illuminating for the discussion in this chapter. For instance, the main finding of these studies has been that inflation under flexible arrangements has been higher and more volatile than under pegged ones. In many countries, however, that correlation emerged due to fiscal indiscipline rather than to an exogenous decision to adopt a flexible exchange rate. Other problems with these studies are difficulties in classifying the regimes, a lack of robustness of results across samples and periods, and the small number of developing countries that have had floating rates for a significant number of years. For a discussion of some of these issues, see Edwards and Savastano (1998).

peg to the Indian rupee. Brunei Darussalam pegs to the Singapore dollar. Other small countries, generally with more diversified trade patterns, peg to currency baskets.

On the basis of the above criteria, another group of countries for which pegged exchange rate regimes would appear relevant, for the future if not necessarily for the near term, are the more advanced transition economies of Central and Eastern Europe that aspire to membership in the European Union and to eventual participation in European Economic and Monetary Union (EMU). The criteria of dominant trading partner (and the benefits of closer economic integration with that partner), as well as willingness to give up monetary independence, are clearly relevant, indeed controlling, in the longer term. For the near to medium term, however, various considerations argue against hard pegs and in favor of more flexible exchange arrangements. Time is needed to strengthen fiscal policies and to address weaknesses in financial sectors and thereby better prepare for full capital market liberalization. It is also important to allow for a possible conflict between exchange rate stability and price stability that may arise because of substantial differences in productivity growth as the transition countries continue to catch up with their more advanced partners (Masson, 1999). Nevertheless, with a view toward their ultimate objective, these EMU aspirant countries will want to lay the firm foundations that are necessary for successful exchange rate pegs by countries substantially open to global financial markets.[37]

Developing countries that face the difficult problem of stabilizing their economies from a situation of high inflation comprise yet a third group for which exchange rate pegs are relevant. As discussed in Appendix III, and contrary to widespread beliefs, exchange-rate-based stabilizations have been used quite successfully by a number of these countries. The key to success in many cases, however, has been in knowing when and how to exit from an exchange rate peg that has done its job in helping to achieve (often dramatic) disinflation with comparatively little economic cost, but which is not sustainable in the longer term.

Beyond these specific groups (which together account for a substantial number of countries), there are a significant number of large, medium-sized, and smaller developing and transition countries for which some form of pegged exchange rate, tight band, crawling band, or heavily managed float is the relevant exchange rate regime. One important example is the largest developing country, China.

China's official exchange rate policy is a managed float, but within that policy, the exchange rate of the yuan has been tightly linked to the U.S. dollar since mid-1995. With a substantial (but recently declining) current account surplus, with large foreign exchange reserves, and with controls that sharply limit short-term capital inflows and outflows, China has maintained its de facto exchange rate peg through all of the turmoil of recent emerging market crises and, thereby, has made an important contribution to the restoration of financial stability in the region. The financial infrastructure for a broad, deep, and resilient foreign exchange market for the Chinese currency does not now exist and would take time to develop (along with other essential improvements in the Chinese financial system). A gradual move to more flexibility in the future, combined with development of the financial infrastructure, would be consistent with other desirable reforms in the Chinese economy.

Other developing countries (of varying economic size) are in situations not too different from that of China, at least with respect to their exchange rate regimes. Without significant involvement in global financial markets, especially for short-term flows, these countries are generally less vulnerable than most emerging market economies to a rapid and massive buildup of speculative pressures against a pegged exchange rate. Often lacking the relevant infrastructure for a viable foreign exchange market that would operate with reasonable stability in the absence of guidance from the authorities, these countries typically either have pegged or heavily managed exchange rates.

Many of these exchange rate regimes can, and do, function reasonably successfully provided that some key conditions are met. The most important concern the nexus between exchange rate policy and monetary policy—the subject of the next subsection. While monetary policy may have some limited flexibility to pursue other objectives, it is essential that the expansion of domestic money and credit do not undermine the exchange rate regime. If significant disequilibria begin to develop between the actual exchange rate and its economically appropriate level, beyond what may be reasonably corrected by other policy adjustments, it is important that decisions to adjust the exchange rate be taken before the necessary adjustment becomes seriously destabilizing. To contain the potential damage from exchange rate adjustments when they are needed, it is also important to ensure that domestic businesses and financial institutions do not take on substantial net foreign-currency liabilities under the incentives created by the quasi-insurance suggested by a pegged exchange rate. This latter task is presumably easier in countries with only limited access to modern, global financial markets.

---

[37] On the pros and cons of currency board arrangements in the lead-up to EU accession, see Gulde and others (2000).

Exchange Rate Pegs as Nominal Anchors

It is important to recognize that for centuries up until the 1970s, except during occasional periods of war or other substantial disruption, the values of all national monies were fundamentally defined by linking their values to some external asset. Gold and silver were the key external assets through the early part of this century. After World War II, under the Bretton Woods system, nations pledged to maintain the values of their currencies within narrow bands of central parities defined against the U.S. dollar, which was pegged (somewhat tenuously) to gold. Only since 1973 have we had an international monetary system in which exchange rates of the national currencies of the three largest industrial countries and some of the medium-sized industrial countries float in response to market pressures without much official guidance. Indeed, most of the medium-sized industrial countries in Europe have eschewed free floating and have instead fastened their exchange rates increasingly tightly to the deutsche mark, and have now moved on to monetary union.

For many developing countries, particularly those with less sophisticated financial systems, it may simply be unreasonable to think that there can be a credible anchor for expectations about monetary policy and for the exchange rate if the authorities do not establish some guide for the value of the money that they create in terms of some readily available alternative asset of stable value. Pegging the exchange rate, or tightly managing its range of variability, is a simple, transparent, and time-honored way of providing such an anchor, and for many developing countries, there may be no readily available alternative.

Pegs, Baskets, Bands, Crawls, and Managed Floats

Pegged exchange rate regimes imply an explicit or understood commitment undertaken by the policy authorities to limit the extent of fluctuation of the exchange rate to a degree that provides a meaningful nominal anchor for private expectations about the behavior of the exchange rate and the requisite supporting behavior of monetary policy. Quite a broad range of regimes share this general characteristic, with a varying degree of permissible exchange rate flexibility, ranging from very hard, single-currency pegs, to basket pegs, to bands, to adjustable pegs and bands, to crawling pegs and bands, to managed floats.

Aside from outright adoption of another country's currency, the hardest form of a pegged exchange rate regime is a currency board (see Box 3.1). Under a currency board, monetary policy is entirely subordi-

nated to the exchange rate regime; and expansions and contractions in the supply of base money (and, therefore, movements in domestic interest rates) are determined by foreign exchange inflows and outflows. These arrangements leave no room for adjustments in the real exchange rate through changes in the nominal exchange rate. Accordingly, adjustments to changing economic conditions affecting the equilibrium real exchange rate, including temporary shocks, must be made by other means, including changes in the levels of domestic prices and costs and (usually short-run) changes in the levels of economic activity and employment. Thus, among the criteria that make a pegged exchange rate regime economically sensible (described above), countries with currency boards must be particularly mindful of the need for flexibility in their economies and in their economic policies (other than exchange rate and monetary policy).

Even for countries that adopt currency boards, as well as for less stringent forms of pegged exchange rate regimes, one way to retain the main anchor properties of an exchange rate peg while gaining some adaptability to one potentially important source of external disturbances—fluctuations among the exchange rates of the major international currencies—is to peg to a currency basket. The weights of the various currencies in the basket could reflect, for example, the geographical composition of the country's trade pattern, or the currency weights of the special drawing right (SDR).[38] Relative to a single-currency peg, this alternative has the advantage of reducing the volatility of the nominal and real effective exchange rate—an advantage that would be relevant primarily for countries with diversified trade patterns vis-à-vis the major currency areas. Basket pegs, however, may reduce the microeconomic and informational benefits of maintaining constant at least one, typically the most important, bilateral exchange rate relevant for price comparisons and economic transactions. Also, basket pegs may be less transparent than single-currency pegs. This may be the case particularly in countries where there is widespread use of a foreign currency, and pegging to that currency has immediate popular understanding. In practice, basket pegs are not used as often as sin-

---

[38] While in practice trade weights are the most common choice, Turnovsky (1982) shows that a trade-weighted basket is not necessarily the optimal choice to stabilize output or attain other reasonable macroeconomic objectives. In a simple macroeconomic model, he finds that other variables that should be taken into account include the elasticity of domestic output with respect to the various exchange rates that make up the basket; and the covariances of the interest rates of the countries whose currencies are included in the basket with the disturbances in the demand for domestic output that are of foreign origin.

Box 3.1. Currency Boards

Currency board arrangements (CBAs) are the strongest form of exchange rate peg short of a currency union or outright dollarization.[1] A currency board is committed to supplying or redeeming its monetary liabilities at a fixed exchange rate, which implies that it must hold foreign reserves at least equal to its total monetary liabilities. Moreover, these are the only terms under which a currency board can exchange monetary liabilities; that is, in its pure form, a currency board cannot extend credit. Under these conditions, even short-term interest rates become completely independent of the will of the domestic monetary authorities: market arbitrage will imply that interest rates are closely linked to those of the anchor currency. CBAs have been in operation in several countries, including Djibouti (since 1949), Brunei Darussalam (since 1967), Hong Kong SAR (since 1983), Argentina (since 1991), Estonia (since 1992), Lithuania (since 1994), Bulgaria (since 1997), and Bosnia and Herzegovina (since 1997).

Just as a CBA is an extreme form of exchange rate peg, the conditions for the operation of a CBA, as well as its advantages and costs, are also those of a fixed exchange rate regime (described in the main text of this section) in a more extreme form.

The key conditions for the successful operation of a CBA, in addition to the usual conditions deemed desirable for a fixed exchange rate regime, are a sound banking system, because the monetary authorities cannot extend credit to banks experiencing difficulties; and a prudent fiscal policy, owing to the prohibition of central bank lending to the government.

The advantages of a CBA include, in particular, the credibility of the economic policy regime. This is evidenced by the narrowing of differentials vis-à-vis the anchor currency throughout the yield curve in most countries that have adopted CBAs. Such credibility results from the high political cost of altering the exchange rate, which—in most existing CBAs—is set by law. In the past, CBAs have often been adopted by small, open economies wishing to curb inflation, and Argentina's recent success in this respect has shown that CBAs can facilitate disinflation in larger economies as well.

The costs of a CBA include the absence of central bank monetary operations to smooth out very short-term interest rate volatility (which implies that banks may experience difficulties) and the absence of a lender of last resort. Indeed, countries with CBAs have often experienced banking collapses, leading some of them to establish limited lender-of-last-resort facilities. Finally, the absence of domestic credit by the central bank implies that seigniorage is lower under a CBA than under a normal peg.

The main differences between a CBA and outright dollarization are that in the former case the country retains its (already low, as noted) seigniorage, whereas in the latter case seigniorage goes to the country of the anchor currency unless special arrangements are made; and that dollarization represents an even more complete renunciation of sovereignty than a CBA does, including the loss of an "exit option" that is preserved under a CBA.

---

[1] For further discussion of currency board arrangements, see the October 1997 *World Economic Outlook*, Bennett (1995), Williamson (1995), and Baliño, Enoch, and others (1997).

---

gle-currency pegs are. Moreover, the popularity of basket pegs, which peaked in the first half of the 1980s, declined during the 1990s (Figure 3.7). This decline probably is related to the fact that basket pegs share many of the characteristics of single-currency pegs, which have also been in decline in the officially reported exchange rate regimes.

Most countries with pegged exchange rate regimes do not fix the rate absolutely, but rather undertake an official commitment to keep the exchange rate from fluctuating beyond some permissible band.[39] This commitment can take the form of a public announcement of a band of admissible values for the exchange rate that the authorities will defend by buying or selling in the market, or there could be a de facto band where the public learns of the government's policy through its actions in the market.[40]

When the inflation rate in a country is substantially above that in the major industrial countries (and an immediate effort to reduce inflation to very

---

[39] The distinction between a peg and a band is somewhat arbitrary, but a peg is often understood as a band in which the margins on either side of the central parity are less than or equal to 2.25 percent. In addition, note that a peg or a band can be fixed, or can be reset periodically in a series of mini devaluations. In the latter case, it is customary to label the peg or band as a "crawling" or a "sliding" peg or band.

[40] In the words of Frankel (1999, p. 5), "[when a central bank] announces a band around a crawling basket peg, it takes a surprisingly large number of daily observations for a market participant to solve the statistical problem, either explicitly or implicitly, of estimating the parameters (the weights in the basket, the rate of the crawl, and the width of the band) and testing the hypothesis that the central bank is abiding by its announced regime. This is particularly true if the central bank does not announce the weights in the basket (as is usually the case) or other parameters. By contrast, market participants can verify the announcement of a simple dollar peg instantly."

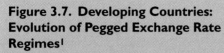

Figure 3.7. Developing Countries: Evolution of Pegged Exchange Rate Regimes[1]
(In percent of total number of developing countries)

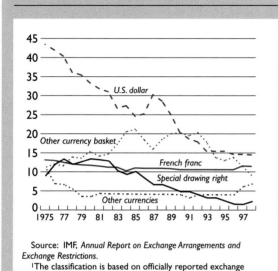

Source: IMF, *Annual Report on Exchange Arrangements and Exchange Restrictions.*
[1]The classification is based on officially reported exchange rate arrangements as of year-end.

low rates is not feasible or desirable), a crawling peg or crawling band becomes a relevant exchange regime option. A *passive* crawling peg or band where the parity is adjusted for past inflation has the virtue that it helps to avoid a tendency for the real exchange rate to appreciate out of line with economic fundamentals, and adjustments to the rate of crawl to correct emerging current account imbalances can be made to deal with changes in real economic fundamentals. The disadvantage of such a regime, however, is that while it may help stabilize the behavior of the exchange rate in the relatively short run, it provides no medium-term nominal anchor. The tendency is to have not a crawling, but rather a "galloping," peg or band that keeps inflation running at a high rate. A strategy that has been used to deal with this problem and to help bring about a gradual disinflation (for example, in Israel since the late 1980s and 1990s and in Poland since the mid-1990s), is to use an *active* crawling peg or band where the rate of crawl is preannounced for up to a year in advance, with the objective of influencing expectations and price-setting behavior.

For an *active* band or crawling band to be useful in stabilizing expectations, however, the authorities must be perceived as having a serious commitment to the arrangement. This, in turn, requires that the authorities face significant costs from abandoning their commitment—costs that are well illustrated by

some initially successful exchange-rate-based stabilizations that subsequently broke down.[41]

Indeed, the principal difficulty of band arrangements, including crawling bands, is that when the exchange rate is driven to the limits of the band (particularly the most depreciated limit), these arrangements work similarly to and can face the same type of problems as standard exchange rate pegs. Especially in the case of emerging market countries with substantial involvement in global capital markets, exchange rate bands are vulnerable to speculative attacks just as currency pegs are. The currencies of Mexico before December 1994, Indonesia before August 1997, and Russia before August 1998 were all in crawling band arrangements. In fact, an exchange rate band may be less credible than a peg is, especially a hard peg such as a currency board, which typically conveys the impression of stronger commitment of monetary policy to the exchange rate regime. Bands typically function best as regimes of policy compromise when there is the readiness to adjust the central parity (or rate of crawl) in a timely manner in response to changing economic fundamentals.

Somewhere along the spectrum of regimes of increasing exchange rate flexibility lie "managed floating" regimes. Unfortunately, a managed float has a sufficiently ambiguous meaning—covering a range of regimes from de facto pegging to something close to a free float. For those managed floats that lie close to the pegging end of the spectrum, the comments that have already been made about various forms of pegged exchange rate regimes continue to apply. There can be some flexibility in the exchange rate, but there must also be a meaningful commitment to defend what the public understands to be the authorities' commitments regarding the exchange rate and related policies. Tightly managed floats provide a nominal anchor and help to stabilize exchange rates and expectations concerning exchange rates, inflation, and monetary policy; but they are subject to market pressures, potential crises, and costly breakdowns.

Monetary Policy Arrangements with Floating Exchange Rates

Under a loosely managed float, market forces are allowed substantial latitude to influence the exchange rate in the short term and in the longer term. Through official intervention and monetary policy adjustments, the authorities may seek to limit exchange rate fluctuations in the near term, but there is no pol-

---

[41] For a discussion of these issues, see Eichengreen, Masson, and others (1998).

icy commitment (explicit or implied) to keep the exchange rate within some range or crawling band. The exchange rate in this case is not a nominal anchor. In these critical respects, loosely managed floats are in the same basic category of exchange rate regimes as free floats. Under the evolving conditions described in the first part of this section, especially the increasing involvement of developing and transition countries in global capital markets, a number of these countries (including emerging market countries) have moved to loosely managed floats.[42]

As the exchange rate does not fulfill the role of nominal anchor in these floating rate regimes, a key issue is how to establish a credible alternative nominal anchor. Institutional arrangements are important in this regard. In particular, central bank independence is important to help mitigate fears that the lack of exchange rate anchor could let loose the money-printing demon.[43] The central bank need not have goal independence, but it should have substantial operational independence (and tenure protection) to pursue an appropriate nominal target that is independent from the financing needs of the public sector and/or from short-sighted considerations associated with the political cycle. Most developing countries have reduced inflation, suggesting that there may be a growing political consensus in these countries that monetary policy should be liberated from these inflationary pressures.

The successful adoption of floating exchange rate arrangements also requires definition of the objective that is to guide the conduct of monetary policy and, accordingly, provide the foundation for private-sector expectations. For this purpose, inflation targeting frameworks such as those adopted in several industrial countries since the early 1990s are likely to receive increasing attention. Under these frameworks, monetary policy is characterized by the announcement of targets for the inflation rate at some low level or range, the periodic assessment of expected inflation over a medium-term horizon, and the systematic adjustment of the monetary policy instrument in order to maintain the relevant inflation measure in line with the target. Inflation targeting frameworks also have often been characterized by increased transparency and accountability of monetary policy, though these features are in principle independent of these frameworks and are desirable in themselves.[44]

An inflation targeting framework allows a degree of discretion and flexibility in the conduct of monetary policy. On the one hand, in practical inflation targeting frameworks, the inflation targets only need to be hit over a medium-term horizon and are often specified in terms of bands rather than point estimates; and in some cases, the central bank reserves the right to make ad hoc adjustments to the inflation measure being targeted (see Bernanke and others, 1999). On the other hand, the emphasis on inflation as the overriding objective of the central bank, and the increased transparency and accountability of monetary policy that often have accompanied the adoption of inflation targeting frameworks, can help to check or limit the degree to which the discretionary powers of the central bank may be used in practice.

Because actual inflation targeting frameworks do not tie the hands of the monetary authority tightly, however, the adoption of such a framework could end up delivering the costs of discretion rather than the benefits of flexibility if it is not implemented properly and if the authorities are not able to demonstrate a commitment to the objective. For this reason, the importance of the institutional developments mentioned above cannot be exaggerated. In particular, a successful inflation targeting framework requires that the central bank be free from the symptoms of fiscal dominance and the pressures imposed by short-term political considerations. The potential costs of discretion also highlight the key importance of technical expertise and judicious central banking for the successful implementation of an inflation targeting framework.[45] Since there are considerable lags in the effect of monetary policy instruments on inflation, it is important to have an effective forecasting procedure that will signal when instrument changes are needed to avoid (prospective) overshoots or undershoots of the target.[46] In addition, relative to the typical industrial country, many developing countries suffer from large supply shocks and have a substantial number of administered prices, which detract, on the one hand, from the predictability of inflation and, on the other, from its controllability. Since it occasionally may be difficult to disentangle the effects on inflation of such shocks from those implied by monetary policy mistakes, the accountability of monetary policymakers under inflation targeting may thus be lower in these countries.

---

[42] For analyses of the float of the Mexican peso, see Edwards and Savastano (1998) and Carstens and Werner (1999).

[43] Many developing countries already have increased the degree of independence of their central banks. See Cottarelli and Giannini (1997).

[44] Countries with inflation targeting regimes include New Zealand, Canada, the United Kingdom, Sweden, and Australia. Analyses of these and some other experiences with inflation targeting are provided in Bernanke and others (1999).

---

[45] The preconditions for the adoption of an inflation targeting framework are discussed in Masson, Savastano, and Sharma (1997).

[46] While some other monetary regimes also require a forecasting procedure, such a procedure is not required under a purely discretionary monetary regime, an exchange rate peg, or a simple money base rule.

An alternative to an inflation target as a nominal anchor under a floating exchange rate regime is to announce targets for the growth rate of some monetary aggregate (or group of aggregates). Such arrangements presumably would be attractive in countries where the relation between monetary growth and inflation is reasonably reliable and where the monetary authorities have relatively good control of the targeted aggregate. However, developing countries seem to rarely meet these conditions. Nevertheless, money growth targets may still be useful if they are an effective means of communicating the intentions of the monetary authorities, with the understanding that the authorities have a responsibility to explain deviations from their announced targets as an essential part of their public accountability. Thought of in this way, money growth targets can be used as a supplement to, rather than a replacement for, inflation targets.[47]

Benign Neglect, Intervention, and Controls

Under all exchange regimes other than absolute free floating, ancillary policy to affect the foreign exchange market through official intervention and controls merits attention. Here, the key point is to recognize that, even for those developing and transition countries for which it is reasonable and appropriate to move toward the floating rate end of the spectrum of exchange arrangements, benign neglect of the exchange rate is unlikely to be a desirable policy. If the foreign exchange market is thin and dominated by a relatively small number of agents, it is likely that the exchange rate will be volatile if the authorities do not provide some guidance and support. This problem is compounded if, as is often the case, there is no long track record of stable macroeconomic policies that can firmly anchor market expectations about the future monetary and exchange rate policy. Also, underdeveloped and incomplete financial markets imply that hedging against exchange rate risk is usually costly and sometimes impossible.[48] As a result, the costs of exchange rate volatility can be substantial for individual agents and for the economy as a whole. In particular, economies with weak financial sector regulation and supervision, and where banks and corporations have a large exposure to foreign-currency borrowing, can be highly vulnerable to unexpected fluctuations in the exchange rate.

Indeed, the facts reveal that developing countries with flexible exchange rate regimes generally do not practice benign neglect of the exchange rate. Compared to the G–3 countries, these developing countries tend to put much more of the weight of the adjustment to macroeconomic shocks on variations in interest rates and in international reserves than on variations in the exchange rate. This is illustrated in Table 3.4, which reports the volatility of the monthly exchange rates, interest rates, and international reserves in selected developing and advanced countries that officially maintained a managed float or an independent float between January 1995 and December 1998. The typical developing country in this category showed during this period a volatility of the exchange rate that was not very different from that observed in industrial countries with floating regimes. However, the volatility of these developing countries' interest rates was substantially larger than the corresponding volatilities in the G–3 rates, as well as typically larger than in those of other advanced countries. Also, the volatility of these developing countries' international reserves tended to be higher than those of the G–3. Thus, the data show that, facing generally larger macroeconomic shocks than the advanced countries, developing countries with flexible exchange rates placed substantially greater importance on the stability of their exchange rates than did the G–3, and significantly greater importance on average than did the other industrial countries with floating rates. Further evidence that developing countries care more about exchange rate fluctuations is provided by the fact that, when measured relative to imports, GDP, and (especially) broad money, their demand for international reserves tends to be much larger than the corresponding demand in industrial country floaters.

From this experience, it is clear that developing countries that maintain relatively flexible exchange rate regimes typically use both monetary policy (interest rate) adjustments and official intervention to influence the exchange rate. Concerning the effectiveness of (sterilized) intervention, it is reasonable to expect that it will generally be more effective in countries where access to international capital markets is limited and, therefore, the authorities have relatively greater capacity to influence conditions in the foreign exchange market by directly buying or selling foreign exchange. For emerging market economies characterized by high international capital mobility, the effectiveness of sterilized interventions is likely to be more limited, or larger interventions will be required to achieve a given effect. The willingness of the central bank

---

[47] A recent survey of the use of explicit targets for monetary policy conducted by the Bank of England (see Sterne, 1999) reports that countries that had both inflation and money targets (and sometimes exchange rate targets as well) substantially exceeded the number of countries that had either only an inflation target or only a money target.

[48] Pegged rates may also have discouraged the development of hedging instruments in the past by underplaying the risk of exchange rate fluctuations.

Table 3.4. Selected Countries with Floating Exchange Rate Arrangements: Volatility of Exchange Rate, Interest Rate, and International Reserves, January 1995–December 1998

	Volatility[1] of			Ratio of Exchange Rate Volatility to		International Reserves		
	Exchange rate[2]	Interest rate	International reserves	Interest rate volatility	International reserve volatility	In months of imports	In percent of GDP	In percent of broad money
Developing countries								
Bolivia[3]	0.3	1.2	6.7	0.3	0.0	5.2	10.9	25.1
Chile[3]	1.6	3.6	3.0	0.4	0.5	8.9	22.2	55.5
Colombia[3]	2.5	6.5	3.0	0.4	0.8	6.0	9.9	49.1
Gambia	0.8	0.1	3.7	6.6	0.2	5.7	25.7	103.1
Ghana	1.8	1.5	11.0	1.2	0.2	2.9	9.5	57.7
India	1.8	0.4	3.9	4.2	0.5	6.8	5.5	12.5
Mauritius[3]	1.8	0.6	4.4	3.2	0.4	3.6	18.7	25.4
Mexico	4.6	9.1	19.7	0.5	0.2	2.5	6.1	23.5
Peru	1.0	4.2	3.4	0.2	0.3	14.2	15.8	73.5
Singapore[3]	2.4	1.0	2.6	2.4	0.9	7.1	81.3	95.2
South Africa	3.2	0.9	20.2	3.6	0.2	1.1	2.4	3.9
Sri Lanka[3]	0.5	13.6	4.7	0.0	0.1	4.3	14.4	45.6
Tanzania	2.4	5.2	19.9	0.5	0.1	3.3	5.5	29.4
Turkey[3]	2.0	9.1	8.1	0.2	0.3	4.7	9.3	36.8
Uruguay[3]	0.7	9.7	6.2	0.1	0.1	3.7	7.1	18.0
Zambia	4.0	2.7	113.1	1.5	0.0	1.9	6.8	42.8
Zimbabwe	5.2	3.9	28.9	1.3	0.2	1.7	5.7	23.6
G-3 countries								
Germany	2.6	0.1	2.3	22.4	1.1	2.1	3.6	6.3
Japan	4.3	0.1	3.0	35.9	1.4	7.5	4.7	4.2
United States	1.5	0.1	3.6	11.2	0.4	0.9	0.8	1.5
Other advanced countries								
Australia	2.5	0.2	6.8	15.9	0.4	2.5	3.7	5.8
Canada	1.4	0.4	7.2	3.3	0.2	1.2	3.1	5.2
Israel[3]	2.2	0.6	5.5	3.5	0.4	2.8	15.9	19.2
New Zealand	2.7	0.7	6.5	4.0	0.4	3.9	7.7	9.2
United Kingdom	1.9	0.3	3.5	5.5	0.5	1.5	3.0	3.0

Sources: IMF, *International Financial Statistics*, and *World Economic Outlook*.

[1]Volatility is defined as the standard deviation of the monthly growth rate of the series for the exchange rate and for international reserves and as the standard deviation of the difference for the interest rate.

[2]Bilateral versus the U.S. dollar for all countries except the United States; nominal effective exchange rate for the United States.

[3]Managed floaters.

and the treasury to support the commitment to defend the exchange rate using their own resources, however, may help to modify the expectations of other market participants (the "signaling channel"), thus affecting also the level of private supply and demand in the market. On the other hand, if private agents come firmly to the conclusion that official efforts to control an exchange rate through intervention—especially intervention unsupported by monetary policy—are unsustainable, large resources to carry out intervention may be viewed as a profit opportunity.

It has already been emphasized that developing and transition countries that maintain significant controls on capital account transactions, and whose

involvement with global financial markets is limited, are typically in a different situation with respect to management of their foreign exchange regimes than are the emerging market countries where involvement is more extensive.[49]

A different issue concerns the use and usefulness of controls by countries that do have significant

---

[49] Capital or foreign exchange controls are, of course, only one of the reasons why a country may lack intensive involvement with global financial markets. Many countries are effectively precluded from such involvement because they are considered too poorly developed economically and financially or because they are perceived as insufficiently creditworthy.

links to global capital markets as part of their exchange rate policy.[50]

Here, it is relevant to distinguish between controls on capital outflows that are imposed to resist downward pressures on the exchange rate and controls on capital inflows that are intended to discourage particular forms of inflows. In the case of the former, the experience with success in the face of substantial and sustained pressures is not particularly encouraging.[51]

It is unclear whether controls on inflows can have much effect in relieving upward pressure on the exchange rate for countries that maintain substantial openness to global financial markets (despite such controls). These controls may, however, be able to influence the composition of capital inflows—for good or ill. Controls that discourage foreign direct investment or longer-term credit inflows may indirectly encourage short-term credit inflows. Controls that seek to discourage short-term credit inflows (which are usually denominated in foreign currency) would tend to shift the composition of inflows in the reverse direction. As discussed in IMF (1995a) and Eichengreen, Mussa, and others (1999), short-term credit inflows pose particular risks of financial crises and of possible systemic defaults, so that measures to shift the composition of international capital flows away from these inflows can help to diminish risks of crisis. To the extent that these measures raise the cost of short-term external indebtedness, they might also, to some extent, facilitate the defense of the exchange rate from the upward pressure stemming from the temporary inflows, while maintaining a degree of independence in the conduct of monetary policy.

Concluding Remarks

For the broad range of developing and transition countries, exchange rates are typically very important macroeconomic variables, and increasingly so because of the trends toward increased involvement of these countries in the global economic system. Reflecting wide differences in levels of economic and financial development and in other aspects of their economic situations, no single exchange rate regime is most appropriate for all such countries, and the regime that is appropriate for a particular country may change over time.[52] Because of their

limited involvement with modern global financial markets, some form of exchange rate peg or band or highly managed float is generally more viable and more appropriate for them than for most of the emerging market countries. Even this conclusion, however, leaves a wide range of possible regimes—for a diverse range of developing and transition countries.

IMF advice to members (including the emerging market countries) on their exchange rate policies (reviewed in Appendix IV) reflects this ambiguity and diversity. Consistent with the Articles of Agreement, the IMF generally respects the member's choice of exchange rate regime and advises on policies needed to support that choice. In the context of IMF-supported programs, changes in exchange rates (such as the devaluation of the CFA franc in 1994), and even changes in exchange rate regimes (such as Bulgaria's adoption of a currency board in 1997), have sometimes been required, along with other policy adjustments. Contrary to some popular misconceptions, recent IMF-supported programs (with Mexico in 1995, and with Asian countries in 1997–98) have typically not involved financing a defense of currency pegs. In cases where a peg was judged sustainable, however, the IMF has provided support (such as recently in Argentina). There have also been cases in which pegs were initially judged sustainable but subsequently had to be abandoned (Brazil in 1999 and Russia in 1998, both of which had crawling pegs). With increased capital mobility, as countries approach emerging market status, the requirements for sustaining exchange rate pegs become more demanding. This suggests that some countries may need to consider an exit strategy from pegged rates earlier than has typically been the case in the past.

Regional Exchange Rate Arrangements

Some important regional groups of emerging market economies—namely the ASEAN and Mercosur countries—are in the situation of having both diversified linkages to the industrial countries and significant intraregional trade. These regional groups face the problem that substantial exchange rate fluctuations within the group, as well as vis-à-vis the industrial countries, can have destabilizing effects and can tend to undermine regional economic cooperation.

One option to address this problem is to consider some form of regional monetary and exchange rate arrangement, following the example of various arrangements (leading up to the creation of EMU) designed to help meet similar concerns of many European countries. The objective of such arrangements presumably would be to avoid or ameliorate

---

[50] On country experiences with the use and liberalization of capital controls, see Ariyoshi and others (2000).

[51] The recent experience of Malaysia, which imposed outflow controls on September 2, 1998, is analyzed in IMF (1998b). In this case, the controls were never really tested in the sense that the exchange rate of the ringgit (like that of the other Asian crisis countries that did not impose controls) was not under significant downward pressure after the controls were imposed.

[52] This is consistent with the conclusion of Jeffrey Frankel (1999) in his recent Graham Lecture on the subject, ". . . no single currency regime is right for all countries at all times."

the sharp swings recently experienced in exchange rates among key members of these regional groups (see Figure 3.8). Such swings may generate political resistance to the goal of intraregional free trade. For example, swings in the real exchange rate between Argentina and Brazil generated substantial protectionist sentiment in these two countries during the early 1990s.[53]

However, formal arrangements to coordinate monetary and exchange rate policies (as in the European example) and limit intraregional exchange rate fluctuations do not seem to be immediately applicable to ASEAN or Mercosur. Neither of these regional groups presently has the institutional structures or the political consensus needed for regional economic integration, including integration of monetary and exchange rate policies, of the kind that took many years to develop in Europe. With less political consensus on the virtues of closer economic integration, and with weaker institutional structures to build upon and develop the implications of such a consensus, it seems doubtful that formal mechanisms for effective intraregional coordination of exchange rate and monetary policies, similar to the European Monetary System (EMS) in Europe, could function effectively in ASEAN and Mercosur at the present time. More ambitious efforts at regional cooperation, such as creation of a common regional currency, are an even more distant prospect. Accordingly, discussion of the economic issues relevant to these approaches is deferred to Appendix V.

For the relatively near term, however, less formal mechanisms for coordinating exchange rate policies may be feasible—probably more so among the ASEAN countries than in Mercosur. Prior to the recent emerging market crises, exchange rate policies among the key ASEAN countries were coordinated de facto by national policies that limited exchange rate fluctuations vis-à-vis the U.S. dollar, with the result that bilateral nominal exchange rates among these countries fluctuated relatively little. Nominal and real effective exchange rates fluctuated somewhat more, reflecting different national inflation rates and different trade weights for various trading partners. Similarly, in Mercosur, before the floating of the Brazilian real in early 1999, fluctuations in the bilateral nominal exchange rate between the real and the Argentine peso were limited by the respective national policies concerning exchange rates vis-à-vis the U.S. dollar.

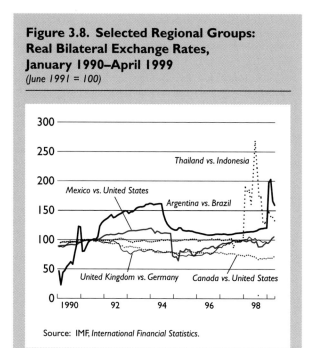

Figure 3.8. Selected Regional Groups: Real Bilateral Exchange Rates, January 1990–April 1999
(June 1991 = 100)

Source: IMF, *International Financial Statistics.*

As recent crises abate, what are the prospects—and the risks—of reestablishing this form of de facto regional exchange rate policy coordination? In the case of Mercosur, Argentina remains dedicated to its convertibility plan, and has rigorously sought to implement the policies and build the institutions that will sustain its currency board. It has also discussed the possibility of moving beyond the currency board by complete dollarization—in effect eliminating the national currency. Brazil, on the other hand, has moved to a floating exchange rate regime, with monetary policy oriented toward an inflation target. This probably means that exchange rates between the two largest Mercosur members will be more volatile than they had been before January 1999, but not as volatile as they had been immediately after the Brazilian real's depreciation or for most of the 20-year period before 1994. Pending developments that may strengthen the basis for regional cooperation on exchange rate policies and other issues in the years to come, the Mercosur countries will need to adapt to a fundamental difference in the exchange rate (and related) policies of the two largest participants. In particular, Argentina must continue to improve the flexibility of its economy—notably (but not only) in its labor markets—to enhance its capacity to adapt to a variety of shocks without exchange rate flexibility.

In ASEAN, the prospects for—and the risks of—returning to implicit exchange rate policy coordina-

---

[53] This is documented in Bevilaqua (1997). See also Eichengreen (1998) for a brief review of this experience. Frankel (1997) finds that, for the ASEAN and Mercosur countries, trade is two or three times greater than proximity, shared languages, and other factors would suggest.

tion by a return to explicit or de facto currency pegs (or quasi-pegs) to the U.S. dollar appear greater than in Mercosur. Malaysia established a formal peg of the ringgit to the U.S. dollar on September 1, 1998. After great turbulence at the height of the Asian crisis, the Thai baht's exchange rate against the U.S. dollar has been relatively stable since late 1998. In view of the still substantial real depreciations of the baht and ringgit as compared with the period just before the Asian crisis, as well as Thailand and Malaysia's large current account surpluses, it seems reasonably likely that their exchange rates will be subject to upward market pressure, especially if the U.S. dollar corrects downward against other major currencies. The Philippines and Indonesia (as well as Korea, which is not in ASEAN) may well be in similar situations.

Resistance to upward pressures on exchange rates (primarily through sterilized intervention) because of concerns about maintaining export competitiveness can become expensive if domestic interest rates rise above world market interest rates. Nevertheless, such efforts can usually be sustained much longer than efforts to defend an exchange rate that is perceived as overvalued. There is no clear limit to the reserves that a country may acquire in efforts to resist exchange rate appreciation; whereas markets know that there is a limit to the reserves available to resist depreciation. There is an important danger, however, in slipping back into de facto pegging of exchange rates against the U.S. dollar. While this may be sustainable for some considerable period, it may well eventually contribute to recreating the problems that led up to the Asian crisis.

To avoid or mitigate this potential problem, it is important for the ASEAN countries (and other east Asian economies including Korea, China, and Taiwan Province of China) to recognize and take appropriate account of their mutual interdependence in the particular context of their exchange rate (and related) policies. If there are general upward pressures on the exchange rates of these economies and only one or two respond by allowing their exchange rates to appreciate, they will tend to lose competitive position relative to those regional partners who aggressively resist exchange rate appreciation. Recognizing this possibility, all will be encouraged to resist exchange rate appreciation even when economic fundamentals point in this direction. In contrast, if there is a general understanding that exchange rates will be allowed to adjust in response to market pressures (although not necessarily with benign neglect), then one country should be less concerned that in responding to such pressures it will be disadvantaged relative to its regional partners and competitors.

There is no easy way of writing formal rules for this loose form of regional cooperation on exchange rate policies. Because different Asian economies were affected differently by recent crises, are recovering in different ways and at different speeds, and remain subject to different domestic and external shocks, market pressures on their exchange rates are unlikely to be uniform. However, it should be feasible to take some account of common factors that are likely to influence these economies in a similar if not identical fashion. In particular, movements in major currency (especially dollar/yen) exchange rates might be taken into account by shifting, on a regional basis, from exchange rate policies that focus heavily on the U.S. dollar to more of a currency basket approach. Also, or alternatively, agreement might be sought to limit exchange market intervention (or the pace and scale of reserve accumulation) in order to ensure that market forces are allowed reasonable latitude, by all of the regional partners, to move exchange rates up and down in response to changing economic conditions. Beyond such possibilities, and pending consideration and possible development of more ambitious efforts at regional exchange rate coordination (discussed in Appendix V), regional cooperation in the near term will need to take a flexible approach, based on mutual understanding and trust, and backed up by regional and international surveillance.

Concluding Remarks

Looking at the diverse circumstances, needs, and preferences of the more than 150 IMF members not categorized as industrial countries, it may fairly be concluded on the basis of the preceding discussion that no single exchange rate regime (and associated policies) may be prescribed as best for all. Nor does this diverse group of countries, in general, face a stark choice between very hard pegs and essentially free floating—although such a choice is probably increasingly pressing for those countries with substantial involvement in modern, global capital markets. Nor is the best choice of exchange rate (and associated policy) regime always clear for many individual countries, even in light of their specific circumstances. There are no simple, universal answers. However, there is a good deal that can reasonably be said about what are likely to be the most appropriate choices of exchange rate regime depending on the circumstances of particular countries.

First, for most emerging market countries, primarily in Asia and Latin America (but also South Africa and some countries in Eastern Europe), floating exchange rate regimes appear to be the increasingly relevant choice. These countries have important and generally expanding involvement with modern global financial markets—with many other developing and transition countries yet to follow in their paths. For these emerging market countries, the tequila crisis of 1995 and the Asian/Russian/Brazilian crises of 1997–98 forcefully illustrated the same lessons learned by the industrial countries in the ERM crises of 1992/93—that the policy requirements for maintaining a pegged exchange rate can be very demanding in circumstances of high international capital mobility. In this situation, several emerging market countries (including Mexico, Peru, and South Africa) successfully maintained floating exchange rate regimes. These regimes appear to have been helpful in handling a variety of economic shocks, including the pressures of recent crises, thereby providing evidence that floating rates are often the most workable regimes for many emerging market countries.

For floating rate regimes to function effectively for such countries and avoid the substantial problems that tend to develop over time with exchange rate pegs, however, it is important that exchange rates actually move—in both directions—in response to market forces, sometimes by significant amounts in short periods. Only such movement can persuade private economic agents to recognize and prudently manage the foreign exchange risks that are inescapable for countries open to global financial markets. This does not imply a policy of benign neglect toward the exchange rate. For emerging market countries that are generally quite open to international trade as well as to global finance, movements in exchange rates have important economic consequences, and it is often appropriate for economic policies, including monetary policies and official exchange market intervention, to take account of and react to exchange rate developments. However, tight management of the exchange rate that provides the convenience of limited exchange rate volatility in normal times also tends to foster dangerous complacency about foreign exchange risks that can suddenly become quite large, as was dramatically illustrated in the Asian crisis. Thus, for emerging market countries that cannot or choose not to undertake the very strict regimen necessary to sustain pegged exchange rate regimes in an environment of international capital mobility, it is essential that floating exchange rates really do float.

Second, for certain emerging market countries, pegged exchange rate regimes and their required supporting policies and institutions can be workable, despite substantial involvement with global financial markets. Notable in this category are countries that have already put in place the policies and institutions needed to support a pegged exchange rate, have established the credibility of those policies and institutions, and have induced appropriate adaptive behavior of the economic and financial system to the

characteristics of the regime. For such countries, in general, the harder and more credible the peg, the better. In contrast, a pegged exchange rate regime that is adopted (de jure or de facto) when conditions are favorable, but without adequate policy commitment and institutional foundation, can become an invitation to costly crisis when conditions turn less favorable. An environment of capital mobility allows massive pressures to be exerted against a pegged exchange rate that, for whatever reasons, has become suspect in the market. To defend the peg, monetary policy must be able to respond forcefully, and the economy and financial system must be able to withstand the strain if the regime is to be credible. Countries that are not adequately prepared to withstand the potential strains of exchange rate defense should beware of slipping into exchange rate pegs that may later foster serious economic and financial crises. And, even for countries with strong foundations, maintenance of pegged exchange rates in a crisis environment can be a demanding endeavor.

Third, beyond the 30 or so "emerging market" economies, the majority of developing and transition economies do not have highly sophisticated domestic financial systems, are not deeply integrated into world capital markets, and (in many cases) maintain fairly extensive controls on capital account (and current account) transactions. These countries currently include a number of the larger and medium-sized developing countries. If inflation in these countries is high because of needs for monetary financing of the fiscal deficit or for other reasons, then exchange rate pegs cannot be sustained for long periods. However, if monetary policy can maintain reasonable discipline, then pegged exchange rate regimes (or bands or crawling pegs or crawling bands) can be viable for extended periods; and, if adjustments are undertaken in a timely manner, they need not be associated with costly crises. Nevertheless, as they become more developed, more financially sophisticated, and more integrated into global financial markets, these countries also will need to consider regimes of greater exchange rate flexibility.

Among the countries for which pegged exchange rate regimes are relevant for the future, if not necessarily in the near term, are the more advanced transition economies of Central and Eastern Europe that aspire to membership in, or close association with, the European Union and European Economic and Monetary Union. Starting from a variety of exchange rate regimes, there is special reason for these countries to build the policy frameworks and institutions that will allow them to sustain hard exchange rate pegs in an environment of high capital account openness.

Many smaller countries that account for only a modest share of world output but are a substantial fraction of the IMF's total membership may also be included in the group of peggers. Even for the most advanced of these small countries seeking to maintain pegged exchange rates, moderate constraints on the development of financial instruments and practices that might facilitate speculation against the peg can probably help, along with disciplined monetary policy, to sustain the exchange rate regime. Moreover, for the many small countries that do maintain pegged exchange rates, the choice of currency to which they peg generally has a sensible and clearly understandable rationale.

Yet another group of countries for which pegged exchange rates offer important attractions are countries that need to stabilize their economies from situations of high inflation. As discussed in Appendix III, there are many examples of successful stabilization from high inflation based on an exchange rate peg. Although there are few countries where high inflation remains a problem, the lessons remain relevant. The main challenge in these endeavors is to recognize that while an exchange rate peg initially may be very useful in the stabilization effort, the exchange rate peg (or crawling peg or band) may not be sustainable in the longer term. Thus, it is very important to know when, and under what circumstances, it may be appropriate to move away from a peg to forestall risks of a major future crisis. This is the issue of "exit" from an exchange rate peg that was discussed intensively in Eichengreen, Masson, and others (1998).

Finally, regional groups of emerging market countries that have both diversified economic linkages to the major currency areas and significant intraregional linkages to other emerging market countries (specifically the ASEAN and Mercosur groups) face particular challenges in devising and managing their exchange rate regimes. Joint pegging of exchange rates to a single major currency (de facto or de jure) has the advantage of coordinating the exchange rate policies among the group, so long as the exchange rate pegs are sustainable. But, as illustrated in recent crises, in addition to the general difficulties of sustaining exchange rate pegs for countries substantially open to global financial markets, this solution is vulnerable both to pressures arising from fluctuations of exchange rates among the major currencies and to the contagion that can arise when the collapse of one country's exchange rate peg calls into question the sustainability of the pegs of other members of the regional group. A joint peg to a basket of major currencies reflecting the trading pattern of the regional group would arguably be a better choice than a single currency peg. More flexible arrangements that use currency baskets as reference points for regional cooperation (rather than as the basis for exchange rate pegs), however, may be better suited to regional groups of countries that are substantially open to modern, global financial markets. More ambitious efforts at regional cooperation on exchange rate arrangements, such as those that have evolved in Europe, merit consideration, but also require a degree of political consensus and institutional development that suggest that they are relevant primarily for the longer term.

IV Concluding Remarks

One main theme of this paper has been that, in the current global economic context, no single exchange rate regime may be prescribed for all countries. However, it is crucial that the chosen exchange rate regime be credibly supported by a set of policies, in particular monetary and fiscal policy, that is fully consistent with the logic of that regime. The particular circumstances of the country and of the times will in turn dictate which policies and regimes are feasible and appropriate. With rising capital mobility and integration into world asset and goods markets, however, an increasing number of countries are moving, and are likely to continue to move, toward the ends of the spectrum that extends from purely floating exchange rates to very hard pegs. This "hollowing of the middle" does not mean that all countries will or should move to the very end of the exchange rate spectrum. In particular, for any but the largest and most advanced countries moving to the floating end of the range of regimes, the behavior of the exchange rate typically will remain a matter for policy concern and intervention may occasionally be appropriate. Neither will the middle be hollow for some time to come. Thus, crawling pegs or bands, for instance, can represent viable alternatives provided, however, that macroeconomic policies be kept consistent with the particular system that is chosen.

Taking a broader view of the evolution of the international monetary system, the advent of the euro and the move of a number of countries toward euro- or dollar-based pegs (possibly as a precursor to full monetary union or dollarization) indicates a trend movement toward a bi-or tri-polar system of major currency areas. At the same time, one would expect a number of countries to maintain basically floating exchange rates toward the major currencies while pursuing efforts at regional monetary cooperation, particularly within the Mercosur and ASEAN groups. The realization of the more ambitious projects for full monetary integration within those groups, however, will become a live option only in the longer run as they require a degree of political cohesion and institutional development that can be forged only over time. In the meantime, the relations among the euro, the dollar, and the yen are likely to be characterized by floating exchange rates that will exhibit a degree of volatility similar to that witnessed in the past few decades. In such a system, the anchor of stability for the system at large will have to remain the macroeconomic policies in the three major currency areas.

Appendix I   Trade Weights and Exchange Rate Volatility

This appendix presents some evidence for the hypothesis that the exchange rates of large, relatively closed economies will tend to be more volatile than those of small, relatively open economies. This is done (a) by relating the volatility of the bilateral nominal exchange rate of a country with a trade partner to the importance (as a share of its GDP) of its trade with that partner (in Table A1.1); and (b) by relating a measure of openness to the volatility of the U.S. dollar and effective nominal and real exchange rates (Table A1.2).

Table A1.1 shows the standard deviations of the growth rates of the (bilateral) exchange rates of 13 countries and the euro area with the U.S. dollar, the deutsche mark, the Japanese yen, and the synthetic euro. The table also shows the share of trade of each of the 13 countries and the euro area with the United States, Germany, Japan, and the euro regions.[54] In general, the bilateral rate with an area representing a small portion of a particular country's trade was more volatile than that with a more important trade partner. The correlation coefficient between volatility as measured here and trade shares was 0.74. Note that in almost all cases the two highest volatilities were found for those two partner countries (or areas) with which the share of trade was lowest. The most notable exception was Australia, a major commodities exporter, where all four volatilities were relatively high. Of course, a decision to target a particular exchange rate parity can override this negative relationship, so that European countries that were members of the European Monetary System (EMS) or that "shadowed the deutsche mark" provide some exceptions. Notably, the European countries—where intraregional trade is generally quite high—all show relatively low volatility with the synthetic euro and the deutsche mark, in comparison with volatility vis-à-vis the dollar and the yen. For visual illustration, Figure A1.1 provides a scatter diagram of the data in Table A1.1, together with the least squares line given by a regression of volatility on trade shares.

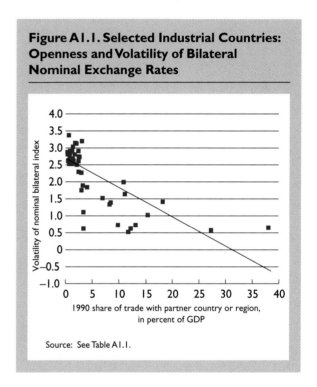

Figure A1.1. Selected Industrial Countries: Openness and Volatility of Bilateral Nominal Exchange Rates

Source: See Table A1.1.

Table A1.2 relates the 1990 proportion of trade to GDP in the 13 countries and the euro area to the volatility of their bilateral U.S. dollar and effective exchange rates over the 1980–98 period. The hypothesis is that the larger the country or the more closed it is, the higher the volatility of its exchange rate. This hypothesis was not borne out for the European countries in the sample for the bilateral U.S. dollar exchange rates, presumably because a large number of these countries were pegging, explicitly or implicitly, for much of the period to the deutsche mark and hence shared that currency's volatility against the U.S. dollar. For Canada, which has quite an open economy and trades predominantly with the United States, the volatility of the bilateral exchange rate with the U.S. dollar was only 30–40 percent of the other volatilities reported in the table. Turning to effective exchange rates, the statistics presented in the table broadly support the hypothesis that exchange rate volatility is inversely related to openness.

---

[54]The 13 countries are Australia, Belgium, Canada, Finland, France, Germany, Italy, Japan, the Netherlands, Sweden, Switzerland, the United Kingdom, and the United States.

Table A1.1. Openness and Volatility[1] of Bilateral Nominal Exchange Rates, June 1973–December 1998

	1990 Trade[2] with (In percent of GDP)	Volatility of Nominal Bilateral Index[3]		1990 Trade[2] with (In percent of GDP)	Volatility of Nominal Bilateral Index[3]
Australia			**Japan**		
United States	2.47	2.29	United States	2.42	2.91
Germany	0.62	3.37	Germany	0.50	2.62
Japan	3.08	3.20	Japan	...	...
Euro area	1.80	3.15	Euro area	1.25	2.53
Belgium-Luxembourg			**Netherlands**		
United States	2.51	2.75	United States	2.63	2.73
Germany	13.08	0.73	Germany	11.73	0.52
Japan	0.99	2.61	Japan	0.90	2.60
Euro area	38.02	0.65	Euro area	27.27	0.58
Canada			**Sweden**		
United States	15.33	1.02	United States	2.11	2.50
Germany	0.48	2.87	Germany	4.07	1.84
Japan	1.39	3.03	Japan	0.86	2.87
Euro area	1.52	2.62	Euro area	11.13	1.64
Finland			**Switzerland**		
United States	1.25	2.53	United States	2.05	3.13
Germany	3.02	1.75	Germany	8.25	1.34
Japan	0.78	2.74	Japan	1.34	2.66
Euro area	6.95	1.52	Euro area	18.15	1.41
France			**United Kingdom**		
United States	1.33	2.68	United States	2.44	2.61
Germany	3.38	1.11	Germany	2.99	2.27
Japan	0.56	2.61	Japan	0.85	2.91
Euro area	9.83	0.73	Euro area	10.89	1.99
Germany			**United States**		
United States	1.73	2.81	United States	...	...
Germany	...	...	Germany	0.42	2.81
Japan	1.04	2.62	Japan	1.23	2.91
Euro area	12.18	0.63	Euro area	1.30	2.56
Italy			**Euro Area**		
United States	1.02	2.61	United States	1.49	2.56
Germany	3.26	1.89	Germany	3.39	0.63
Japan	0.38	2.88	Japan	0.71	2.53
Euro area	8.47	1.39	Euro area	...	...

Sources: IMF, *Direction of Trade Statistics*, *World Economic Outlook* database, and *International Financial Statistics*.

[1] Volatility is measured by the standard deviation of the growth rate (defined as the difference of the natural logarithm) of the series.

[2] Trade is defined as the average of the country's exports to and imports from the partner country or area.

[3] The bilateral exchange rate indices (average of 1990 = 100) are monthly series from June 1973 to December 1998.

Table A1.2. Selected Industrial Countries: Openness and Volatility of Bilateral and Effective Exchange Rates, February 1980–December 1998

| | 1990 Proportion of Trade in GDP[2] | Volatility of Bilateral Exchange Rate vs. U.S. dollar[1] | | Volatility of Effective Exchange Rates[1] | | | | | |
| | | | | Whole Period | | 1980M2–1987M3 | | 1987M4–1998M12 | |
		Nominal	Real	Nominal	Real	Nominal	Real	Nominal	Real
Belgium-Luxembourg	69.8	2.85	2.81	0.82	0.84	1.00	1.02	0.69	0.70
Netherlands	45.4	2.83	2.82	0.73	0.75	0.80	0.82	0.68	0.70
Switzerland	29.1	3.18	3.13	1.38	1.37	1.46	1.41	1.32	1.34
Germany	25.0	2.84	2.79	0.90	0.91	0.99	1.01	0.87	0.87
Sweden	24.3	2.58	2.63	1.55	1.62	1.56	1.64	1.54	1.61
Canada	21.8	1.02	1.11	1.17	1.25	1.04	1.10	1.25	1.33
United Kingdom	20.8	2.73	2.81	1.83	1.86	2.04	2.08	1.69	1.70
Finland	19.8	2.77	2.78	1.38	1.40	0.88	0.96	1.61	1.61
France	18.8	2.79	2.74	0.89	0.88	1.08	1.10	0.73	0.71
Italy	16.1	2.73	2.69	1.37	1.38	0.81	0.80	1.62	1.63
Australia	13.8	2.33	2.35	2.36	2.31	2.55	2.47	2.23	2.20
Euro Area	10.9	2.71	2.66	1.57	1.57	1.76	1.78	1.45	1.43
Japan	8.8	3.06	3.15	2.52	2.52	2.35	2.39	2.57	2.58
United States	7.9	...	...	1.68	1.67	1.89	1.90	1.54	1.52

Sources: IMF, Information Notice System, *International Financial Statistics*, and *World Economic Outlook* database.

[1] All effective exchange rates are based on U.S. dollar per national currency bilateral rates. Volatility is measured by the standard deviation of the growth rate (defined as the difference of the natural logarithm) of the series. The series are monthly from February 1980 to December 1998.

[2] The average of exports and imports in percent of GDP for the year 1990.

Appendix II Exchange Rate Arrangements of Small Economies

Reflecting different structural characteristics, the exchange rate arrangements of small economies have evolved somewhat differently from those of larger economies. This appendix reviews the exchange rate arrangements used in small economies and examines some of the factors that have influenced, and will continue to influence, the choice of those arrangements. It highlights that the majority of these economies probably will maintain pegged exchange rate regimes, most typically by pegging to a single currency.

Table A2.1 shows the distribution of exchange rate arrangements and other selected data for the 73 IMF members that had a level of GDP of less than $5 billion in 1997.[55] These economies include many island states or territories in the Caribbean, the Pacific, the Indian, and the Atlantic Oceans, as well as numerous small or less-developed continental countries in Africa and elsewhere. As shown in the table, some of these small economies let their exchange rates float, but most maintain pegged exchange rates. In the latter cases, the exchange rate typically is set in terms of a single currency such as the U.S. dollar or the French franc, though a basket of currencies is sometimes used.

The high degree of trade openness of these economies is expected to, if anything, increase further in coming years, tending to reinforce the predominance of pegs in these countries. The key consideration for these highly open economies is that, where trade in goods and services represents a large fraction of domestic production and consumption, the microeconomic benefits of reducing transaction costs and exchange rate risks by pegging the exchange rate can be substantial. In addition, if the tradable sector of the economy is large, domestic wages and prices are likely to react more quickly to changes in the nominal exchange rate. This effect makes it more difficult to modify the real exchange rate through changes in the nominal exchange rate, which instead mostly destabilize domestic prices.

Furthermore, although increased capital mobility may pose a problem for the maintenance of currency pegs in some small economies, most of these economies are not yet closely integrated into international private capital markets. Consequently, the possibility of sudden and massive speculative attacks—such as those that have been observed in some bigger and more advanced economies—remains limited. Even with an open capital account, the fact that such open economies have no incentive to engineer an inflationary surprise enhances the credibility of their pegs. Small economies that maintain pegs that are inconsistent with their macroeconomic policies, however, will still be exposed to damaging currency crashes.

It is also probable that the majority of these economies will continue to peg their exchange rates to a single foreign currency. Many small economies have a large trade partner that provides an obvious standard of reference for setting the peg, and/or are highly dependent on tourism receipts from visitors that use or have easy access to a strong and internationally liquid foreign currency. Pegging the exchange rate to the single most relevant currency not only provides such an economy with a simple and transparent nominal anchor, but also helps to minimize potentially large transaction costs and exchange rate risks. Another relevant consideration is that some small economies have strong political and cultural links with the country that issues the reference currency.

For many small economies, however, the lack of an obvious candidate for a single currency peg will make it preferable to continue to peg to a currency basket or to let the exchange rate float. This will be the case especially for small economies with highly diversified economic and political relations with the rest of the world, and with tourism receipts that do not represent an important share of their exports. It may also be the case for a small economy with a large trade partner that does not have a sufficiently stable and liquid currency.

Small economies with floating exchange rates are typically somewhat larger than small economies with pegged exchange rates. This is consistent with

---

[55]Data for the individual economies underlying Table A2.1 are presented in Table A2.2.

Table A2.1. Small Economies[1]: Distribution of Exchange Rate Arrangements and Selected Indicators

(1998 unless otherwise indicated)

Exchange Rate Arrangement	Number of Countries	Average Size of Economy	Average Trade Share[2]	Average Share of Largest Export Partner[3]	Average Share of Tourism Receipts in Percent of Exports[4]	Fraction of Countries with Controls on Current Account[4]
Pegged	45	1.58	51.8	33.6	18.9	0.78
Peg to single currency	37	1.56	51.4	33.4	16.1	0.81
U.S. dollar	16	1.20	61.1	29.5	37.2	0.69
French franc	13	2.03	34.4	36.9	7.6	1.00
Other	8	1.52	63.4	37.2	8.3	0.75
Peg to basket of currencies	8	1.68	53.4	34.1	28.9	0.63
Flexible	28	2.15	51.3	34.3	9.2	0.57
Managed float	11	2.00	69.7	27.7	7.2	0.64
Independent float	17	2.25	38.7	38.9	10.5	0.53
Memorandum item:						
Small economies	73	1.80	51.6	33.9	11.5	0.70

Source: Based on Table A2.2.

[1] Countries with estimated nominal GDP less than $5 billion in 1998 (subject to availability of data from the *World Economic Outlook*).

[2] Average of exports and imports in percent of GDP.

[3] Largest exports as a share of total exports.

[4] As of 1997.

the fact that the costs of the institutions and the technical expertise required for a well-behaved independent monetary policy and an efficient domestic financial market grow less than proportionally with the size of the economy. For some small economies, it is apparent that these costs can be too high, or even prohibitive, relative to the potential benefits of exchange rate flexibility.

It is important to note that most of the small economies in Tables A2.1 and A2.2 maintain restrictions on current account payments. These restrictions are especially frequent among those small economies that have pegged exchange rates. The lack of currency convertibility in these economies contradicts the fact that small economies are likely to benefit the most by having a high degree of economic integration to the rest of the world. Accepting the obligations of Article VIII of the IMF's Articles of Agreement remains a key challenge for most small economies.

The threshold of $5 billion for GDP is of course arbitrary and increasing it to, say, $20 billion would add a further set of 18 peggers (to a single currency or to a basket) and 24 countries with more flexible arrangements. The peggers include Iceland and Luxembourg among the industrial countries. Iceland pegs to a basket of currencies, while Luxembourg has had a pegged rate for most of the last century, in the form of a monetary union with Belgium. The extent of Luxembourg's goods and labor market integration with its larger neighbor have made a pegged rate both desirable and sustainable, despite the presence of a high degree of capital mobility.

Table A2.2. Small Economies[1]: Exchange Rate Arrangements and Selected Indicators
(1998 unless otherwise indicated)

	Size of Economy (In billions of U.S. dollars)	Trade as Share of GDP[2]	Largest Export Partner		Tourism Receipts in Percent of Exports[5]	Controls on Current Account[5]
			Share[3]	Partner country[4]		
Pegged to the U.S. dollar						
Antigua and Barbuda	0.61	87.0	18.8	Spain	...	1
Bahamas, The	4.12	52.0	22.7	United States	80.0	1
Barbados	2.33	58.4	14.3	United Kingdom	...	1
Belize	0.67	53.0	28.9	United States	27.8	1
Djibouti	0.53	51.4	38.3	Somalia	1.7	0
Dominica	0.25	56.8	22.5	United Kingdom	31.4	1
Grenada	2.30	10.3	30.0	United States	...	1
Liberia[6]	3.07	30.4	27.4	Singapore	...	0
Maldives[6]	0.40	117.0	32.4	United States	68.7	0
Marshall Islands	0.10	...	...	...	...	0
Micronesia, Fed. States of	0.21	...	...	...	0.0	0
Netherlands Antilles	2.51	66.5	17.5	United States	...	1
St. Kitts and Nevis	0.29	60.9	60.3	United States	50.7	1
St. Lucia	0.68	70.1	51.9	United Kingdom	...	1
St. Vincent and the Grenadines	0.30	57.9	31.3	United Kingdom	...	1
Suriname[6]	0.82	83.7	16.2	United States	...	1
Pegged to the French franc						
Benin	2.32	27.8	23.4	Brazil	5.5	1
Burkina Faso	2.54	38.4	67.2	Côte d'Ivoire	7.8	1
Central African Republic	1.06	27.2	42.5	Belgium	2.3	1
Chad	1.67	25.8	24.4	Germany	3.3	1
Comoros	0.19	28.6	62.1	France	46.0	1
Congo, Republic of	1.99	96.2	86.7	United States	0.2	1
Equatorial Guinea	0.46	88.7	87.6	United States	0.5	1
Gabon	4.57	70.6	75.0	United States	0.2	1
Guinea-Bissau	0.20	62.5	85.0	India	...	1
Mali	2.65	28.7	21.8	Italy	3.3	1
Niger	2.01	18.9	68.3	France	6.0	1
Senegal	4.86	34.5	21.5	France	10.8	1
Togo	1.51	37.1	11.3	Canada	2.1	1
Pegged to other currency						
Bhutan[7]	0.36	53.7	...	...	4.9	1
Brunei Darussalam[8]	4.86	50.2	51.4	Japan	...	1
Cape Verde[9]	0.50	46.7	89.3	Portugal	11.4	1
Kiribati[10]	0.06	72.6	21.3	Japan	15.4	0
Lesotho[11]	0.83	116.1	...	...	10.9	0
Namibia[11]	2.99	60.0	...	...	11.1	1
San Marino[12]	...	...	...	...	...	0
Swaziland[11]	1.18	99.8	12.8	South Africa	3.4	1
Pegged to a currency basket						
Botswana	5.11	40.3	...	...	...	0
Burundi	0.98	10.2	34.9	Germany	1.0	1
Fiji	2.33	58.5	32.1	Australia	25.6	1
Malta	3.99	96.3	18.0	United States	23.2	1
Samoa	0.21	43.0	51.1	Australia	50.3	1
Seychelles	0.56	69.5	22.1	United Kingdom	34.2	0
Tonga	0.17	49.4	50.3	India	28.6	1
Vanuatu	0.25	53.6	30.5	Japan	39.5	0
Flexible arrangements:						
Other managed float						
Azerbaijan	4.10	42.5	23.7	Iran	13.8	1
Kyrgyz Republic	1.87	48.8	25.0	Germany	0.6	0
Lao PDR	1.11	51.5	13.0	Thailand	12.9	0
Macedonia FYR	3.25	52.0	20.5	Germany	...	1
Malawi	1.69	40.2	14.4	South Africa	1.1	1

Table A2.2. *(concluded)*

	Size of Economy (In billions of U.S. dollars)	Trade as Share of GDP[2]	Largest Export Partner		Tourism Receipts in Percent of Exports[5]	Controls on Current Account[5]
			Share[3]	Partner country[4]		
Mauritania	0.90	71.9	18.2	Japan	2.4	1
Mauritius	4.03	62.4	30.5	United Kingdom	18.0	0
Nicaragua	2.07	30.2	54.5	United States	9.3	0
Solomon Islands	0.32	82.4	36.0	Japan	5.4	1
Tajikistan	0.98	83.8	46.4	Uzbekistan	...	1
Turkmenistan	1.64	201.2	22.0	Iran	0.9	1
Flexible arrangements:						
Independent float						
Albania	3.94	20.1	59.4	Italy	4.5	0
Armenia	1.86	37.1	23.2	Belgium	3.6	0
Eritrea	0.65	34.1	...	...	37.2	1
Gambia, The	0.41	54.5	72.8	Belgium	9.6	0
Guinea	3.83	21.5	14.9	United States	0.7	1
Guyana	0.74	103.4	25.2	Canada	...	0
Haiti	3.89	15.3	86.3	United States	36.6	0
Madagascar	3.75	25.0	45.7	France	8.7	0
Moldova	2.25	55.6	50.5	Russia	3.3	1
Mongolia	1.06	52.2	49.5	China, PR Mainland	4.4	0
Mozambique	3.89	28.7	17.1	Spain	...	0
Papua New Guinea	3.70	63.7	18.7	Australia	2.9	1
Rwanda	2.08	13.8	32.9	Belgium	0.7	1
São Tomé and Príncipe	0.04	66.6	85.9	Netherlands	32.3	1
Sierra Leone	0.65	26.7	33.5	Belgium	10.9	1
Somalia	2.16	16.4	59.8	Saudi Arabia	...	1
Zambia	3.35	33.8	10.3	Saudi Arabia	5.1	0

Memorandum Item: Fraction of countries with controls

Small economies	0.67
Industrial countries	0.00
Other developing countries	0.59
Other transition countries	0.44

Sources: IMF, *World Economic Outlook, Direction of Trade Statistics, Annual Report on Exchange Arrangements and Exchange Restrictions,* and country desks; World Bank, *World Development Indicators.*

[1]Countries with estimated nominal GDP less than $5 billion in 1998 (subject to availability of data from the *World Economic Outlook*).

[2]Average of exports and imports in percent of GDP.

[3]Country's largest exports as a share of total exports.

[4]Partner country for largest exports.

[5]As of 1997.

[6]Country officially reports a managed or independent float.

[7]Pegged to the Indian rupee.

[8]Pegged to the Singapore dollar.

[9]Pegged to the Portuguese escudo.

[10]Pegged to the Australian dollar.

[11]Pegged to the South African rand.

[12]Pegged to the Italian lira.

Appendix III   Recent Experience with Exchange-Rate-Based Stabilizations

Since the late 1980s, a significant number of developing countries have undertaken *exchange-rate-based stabilization programs*—that is, disinflation programs that included preannounced limits on nominal exchange rate movements. Major programs of this type were implemented in several Latin American economies with histories of chronically high inflation, as well as in many transition economies that had suffered dramatic increases in inflation following the collapse of central planning. A list of these stabilization programs for the countries where 12-month inflation at the beginning of the program exceeded 100 percent is presented in Table A3.1. The experiences with these programs has tended to confirm the benefits and pitfalls of using the exchange rate as the nominal anchor for reducing high inflation.[56]

All of these programs had remarkable success in reducing inflation from extremely high levels (see Table A3.1). After their implementation, the stabilizing effect of the exchange rate commitment on prices and expectations typically permitted inflation to be reduced rapidly, and by the third year of the program annual inflation in most cases had reached single-digit rates. Moreover, these gains in disinflation have been sustained, with inflation typically falling further subsequently. Even in those cases where the exchange rate commitment was abandoned, inflation remains substantially lower than it was before the start of the program.

As in earlier exchange-rate-based stabilization programs, disinflation during recent programs was generally accompanied by rapid real economic growth (see Figure A3.1). In most cases, this phenomenon is explained more by the timing of the programs than by aggregate demand and supply effects induced by the stabilization itself: the programs typically were launched after a period of one or more years of recession or stagnation, and they generally followed or coincided with major structural reforms, which were especially radical in the transition economies. Nonetheless, the persistence of rapid real output growth during the recent programs is consistent with the evidence from earlier programs that stabilizations from high inflation that rely on the exchange rate as the nominal anchor tend to be expansionary.[57]

The recent exchange-rate-based stabilizations also confirm the risks that can be associated with this disinflation strategy (see Figure A3.1). In all countries there was a marked tendency during the first three years of the program for the domestic currency to appreciate in real terms, with a concomitant increase in the external current account deficit. This increase was generally financed by substantial capital inflows, partly attracted by the restoration of investor confidence and the expectation that the exchange rate commitment would be honored at least in the near future. These capital inflows often permitted international reserves to be maintained or even increased, but in general they implied a considerable buildup in external liabilities. As a result, the economies implementing these programs became increasingly dependent on international capital markets and more vulnerable to sudden reversals in capital flows.

In this context of heightened external vulnerability, inconsistencies between economic policies and the exchange rate regime led in some cases to severe currency crises, including the collapse of the Mexican peso in December 1994, the Russian ruble in August 1998, and the Brazilian real in January 1999. In each of these cases, a combination of domestic and external factors led to the attack on and subsequent devaluation of the domestic currency, but policy slippages invariably played an important role. In

---

Note: This appendix is taken from the May 1999 *World Economic Outlook* (IMF, 1999).

[56]For a recent review of the theoretical and empirical literature on exchange-rate-based stabilization, see Calvo and Végh (1999). Most of that literature focuses on stabilizations undertaken until the mid-1980s. See also IMF (1996).

[57]The expansionary effects of exchange-rate-based stabilization programs have been attributed to demand effects resulting from inflation inertia, lack of credibility, and the timing of the purchases of consumer durables, and to supply effects stemming from the response of labor supply and investment. For details, see Calvo and Végh (1999).

Table A3.1. Major Exchange-Rate-Based Stabilization Programs
(Since the late 1980s[1])

| Country | Beginning Date | Exchange Rate Arrangement[2] | Twelve-Month Inflation | | Did the Program End in a Currency Crash? |
			At start of program	Third year of program	In 1998	
Mexico	December 1987	Peg, crawling peg, widening band	143.7	29.9	18.6	Yes (December 1994)
Poland	January 1990	Peg, crawling peg, crawling band	639.6	39.8	8.6	No
Uruguay	December 1990	Crawling band	129.8	52.9	8.6	No
Nicaragua	March 1991	Peg, crawling peg	20,234.3	3.4	...	No
Argentina	April 1991	Currency board	267.0	4.3	0.7	No
Estonia	June 1992	Currency board	1,085.7	29.2	4.4	No
Croatia	October 1993	Asymmetric peg, managed float	1,869.5	4.0	5.3	No
Lithuania	April 1994	Currency board	188.8	8.4	2.4	No
Brazil	July 1994	Peg, crawling peg	4,922.6	6.1	0.4	Yes (January 1999)
Russia	July 1995	Band, crawling band	226.0	5.5	66.8[3]	Yes (August 1998)
Bulgaria	July 1997	Currency board	1,471.9	...	3.2[3]	No

Sources: National authorities; and IMF staff estimates.

[1]In countries where the 12-month inflation rate was above 100 percent at the beginning of the stabilization program.

[2]Where more than one arrangement is listed, the sequence of arrangements is indicated.

[3]November 1997–November 1998.

Figure A3.1. Recent Exchange-Rate-Based Stabilizations: Selected Economic Indicators[1]

(Centered on the year of stabilization)

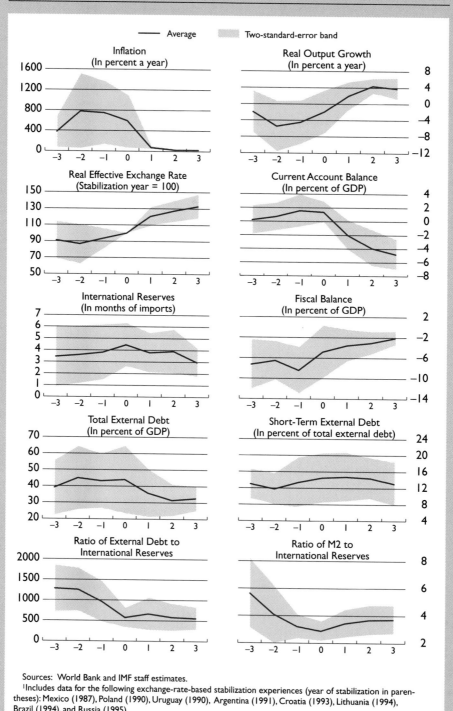

Sources: World Bank and IMF staff estimates.

[1]Includes data for the following exchange-rate-based stabilization experiences (year of stabilization in parentheses): Mexico (1987), Poland (1990), Uruguay (1990), Argentina (1991), Croatia (1993), Lithuania (1994), Brazil (1994), and Russia (1995).

Mexico, the crisis came after a period of accommodating monetary policy and a strong expansion of credit that was inconsistent with the exchange rate anchor.[58] In Russia, the failure for many years to bring the fiscal situation under control led to levels of public debt and debt-service payments that became increasingly unsustainable. And in Brazil, the efforts of the government to cut the public-sector deficit and reduce the public debt encountered opposition and delays in the Congress. All these crises were very costly in terms of their effects on the authorities' credibility, with rising inflation and plummeting output following the devaluations.

Most of the recent programs, however, did not end in a currency crash.[59] In half of the countries that did not experience a currency crash, the consistency of economic policies and the exchange rate regime was ensured by the constraints imposed by the adoption of *currency board arrangements*, which, in addition to fixing the value of the exchange rate, limit the issuance of domestic currency to the amount that can be covered by the central bank's holdings of foreign exchange. This type of monetary and exchange rate arrangement was adopted by Argentina, Estonia, Lithuania, and, more recently, Bulgaria. The currency boards implemented in these countries all remain in place, confirming that the decision to adopt such an arrangement should be made not only from the perspective of short-run inflation stabilization, but also taking into account the medium- or long-run consequences of the inability to implement an independent monetary policy after the stabilization is accomplished.[60]

In the other half of the countries that did not experience a currency crash, the consistency of macroeconomic policies was attained in part by accepting some degree of exchange rate flexibility. In Poland, for instance, the exchange rate regime during the stabilization started as a fixed peg to the U.S. dollar but was later modified, first to a fixed peg to a basket of currencies, then to a preannounced crawling peg, and subsequently to a preannounced crawling band with ±7 percent margins. To varying degrees, the stabilizations in Uruguay, Nicaragua, and Croatia also allowed for some degree of exchange rate flexibility, either by design of the exchange rate regime adopted at the beginning of the stabilization or by subsequent revisions of the original regime as stabilization progressed.[61] Without supporting economic policies, however, the introduction of some degree of exchange rate flexibility was generally insufficient to prevent a currency crash. Before their collapse, the exchange rate regimes in Mexico, Russia, and Brazil had all been made more flexible, although not sufficiently so to avoid a crisis resulting from other policy shortcomings.[62]

To summarize, recent experiences with exchange-rate-based stabilization programs confirm that they can be very effective in stopping high inflation, and that economic performance can improve significantly soon after the program launch. It is key, however, that disciplined macroeconomic policies be implemented while the exchange rate anchor is in place. In addition, a decision will need to be made on whether a longer-term, binding commitment should be made to a fixed exchange rate, or whether some degree of exchange rate flexibility should be allowed after a while. In the latter case, the degree of flexibility should be sufficient to be consistent with the fiscal and monetary policies being implemented.

---

[58]The Mexican crisis was discussed in detail in Annex I of IMF (1995c), and in Chapters II and III of IMF (1995a).

[59]Defined as a nominal depreciation of the domestic currency of at least 25 percent in a year, along with a 10 percent increase from the previous year in the rate of depreciation. This definition is similar to the one used in Frankel and Rose (1996); it excludes instances where a currency came under severe pressure but the authorities were able to defend it.

[60]For a review of currency board arrangements, see Baliño, Enoch, and others (1997).

[61]These revisions typically pointed toward accepting greater exchange rate flexibility. In Croatia, however, the replacement of an original ceiling on the nominal exchange rate by a noncommittal managed-float regime did not imply greater volatility in the exchange rate. Also, the exchange rate band in Uruguay recently was narrowed (in April 1998).

[62]For a discussion of methods for moving to greater exchange rate flexibility under alternative circumstances, see Eichengreen, Masson, and others (1998).

Appendix IV   IMF Advice on Exchange Rate Policy

In recent years, some external observers have criticized the IMF because it appeared to unduly favor fixed exchange rates, others because it appeared to show an inordinate fondness for currency devaluation, and yet others because it appeared to have no principles guiding its advice on exchange rate regimes.[63] The coexistence of these criticisms, which cannot all be valid at the same time, reveals the extent of confusion about the IMF advice on exchange rate policy. This appendix reviews the advice given to member countries.[64]

Consistent with Article IV of the IMF's Articles of Agreement, the usual approach taken by the IMF on this matter has been to abide by a member country's preferred exchange rate regime and to tailor its overall policy advice accordingly. True, discussions about the appropriate exchange rate policy and, in particular, the dismantling of exchange rate restrictions (an area that falls under the direct purview of the IMF as stated in Article VIII of the Articles of Agreement) may be important and, at times, central aspects of program negotiations and surveillance discussions. Moreover, in some cases, the reform of the foreign exchange system or an exchange rate devaluation becomes a precondition for Board approval of an IMF arrangement. But if a country shows a strong preference for a particular exchange rate regime, the usual approach followed by the IMF is to accept the country's choice and then provide policy advice that is consistent with the maintenance of the chosen regime. In countries where a particular exchange rate regime rules out changes in the exchange rate, the IMF advises that the burden of any adjustment required must fall on other policies. Where a change in the exchange rate is possible, the IMF may recommend that appropriate economic and financial policies be used in combination with increased exchange rate flexibility.

The substantial deference that the IMF gives to national authorities in their choice of exchange rate regime reflects both idiosyncratic and broader factors. From the IMF's operational viewpoint, these factors include the need to respect the right of members to determine their own exchange rate arrangement—as established by Article IV of the IMF's Articles of Agreement—and experience showing that IMF programs tend to perform best when their associated policies are most closely "owned" by the national authorities in charge of implementing them. From a broader perspective, in turn, the advice that the IMF can provide on this matter is naturally bound by the lack of agreement in the economics profession about how to determine the appropriate exchange rate regime when the choice is other than obvious. Indeed, it must be recognized that while so far economic science has developed a number of criteria that seem relevant for the choice of exchange rate regime, there is no agreement on how precisely to quantify the various criteria or, to the extent that they conflict, on how to decide which should take priority.[65]

There have been many episodes since the breakdown of the Bretton Woods system of fixed exchange rates that reveal the IMF's typical practice of abiding by a country's preferred exchange rate regime. A vivid example is provided by the many arrangements approved for countries in the CFA franc zone in the years preceding the January 1994 devaluation of the CFA franc—a period when IMF staff voiced repeatedly, though subtly, its concern about the harmful effects of maintaining the old parity. (In some cases, however, the negotiations on the policies needed to address these concerns implied delays in the approval of arrangements with some countries in the region.)

---

[63]The latter criticism, for instance, is illustrated by the following passage from a recent editorial of the *Wall Street Journal* (11/21/97) that stated: "take the very important question of what kind of foreign exchange rate regime an IMF client nation will be advised to follow. This is the kind of thing investors need to know. Well, good luck parsing the guiding principles. The IMF supports Hong Kong's peg to the dollar, and in 1995 actually rode to the rescue of Argentina's peso by supporting a currency board. But for some reason, the IMF favors floats in Southeast Asia. How the IMF decides in a given case is anyone's guess. Do they do it with dartboards? Dice? Computers? Does [former] Managing Director Michel Camdessus flip a coin?"

[64]This appendix draws partly on Mussa and Savastano (1999).

[65]Most of these criteria are discussed in the main body of the text. A systematic presentation can also be found in Appendix I of Eichengreen, Masson, and others (1998).

Many other examples are provided by a large number of IMF arrangements approved in the 1980s that were examined in an external evaluation of IMF conditionality and that led the evaluators to conclude, with some surprise, that "perhaps the strongest tendency of IMF conditionality was to leave existing exchange rate policies intact."[66]

In recent years, the views of country authorities have continued to play the key role in shaping the course of exchange rate policy in IMF-supported programs. For example, Argentina made its own decision to adopt a currency board in early 1991, and received explicit support from the IMF in the form of a stand-by arrangement only in July of that year. When the peg came under intense pressure in the tequila crisis of 1995, a new program supported by the IMF helped Argentina sustain its decision to persevere with its currency board. Similarly, in mid-December 1994, Mexico devalued the peso and then moved to a floating rate system before reaching any agreement with the IMF. Also outside of any IMF arrangement, Brazil adopted the Real Plan in mid-1994 and defended it against intense pressures resulting from the tequila crisis and from the contagion effects of the Asian crisis beginning in October 1997. When Brazil requested, negotiated, and agreed on a program supported by the IMF in November 1998, the decision to continue with the Real Plan (without changing the exchange rate or modifying its rate of crawl) was fundamentally a decision of the Brazilian authorities. As market pressures intensified in mid-January 1999, the decision to devalue the real and subsequently to let it float was again a decision taken by the Brazilian authorities, although with the knowledge that the IMF and the international community probably would not continue to support an exchange rate policy that had become unsustainable in the face of declining market confidence and massive outflows of reserves.

Of course, accepting a country's preferred exchange rate regime does not prevent the IMF from offering the authorities an assessment of whether the prevailing exchange rate is broadly consistent with the country's external and domestic policy goals, nor from recommending policy changes that may be required in order to ensure such consistency. In fact, since providing this type of advice is at the core of the IMF's surveillance and use of resources responsibilities, the staff pays considerable attention to the sustainability of the exchange rate policy followed in countries where the authorities are committed to defend a particular path for the exchange rate, as well as to the possibility of misalignments in the observed level of the exchange rate in countries that let the exchange rate float. For that purpose, IMF staff routinely examines a wide range of economic indicators for each member country—either in the context of surveillance or when negotiating and monitoring IMF arrangements—and analyzes them in the light of the country's structural characteristics, the international context, and the accumulated knowledge of exchange rate issues. In recent years, in addition to traditional domestic and external sector indicators such as the fiscal deficit, monetary or domestic credit growth, the real exchange rate, international reserves, the current account, and several others, the staff has started to pay increasing attention to indicators in the financial sector and the capital account.[67]

In the case of IMF-supported programs, the IMF lends to a country defending a peg or some type of exchange rate commitment only if its ex ante assessment is that such a policy is sustainable under the conditions of the program. It is true that in some cases, such as in Russia in 1998 and in Brazil in 1999, the ex post result has been that the peg or commitment was abandoned, typically in the context of significant policy slippages that implied that the program was not implemented as agreed. In the vast majority of the above cases, however, the lending support provided by the IMF to countries maintaining or defending pegs has permitted them to restore external viability without exposure to currency crashes. For instance, in the IMF arrangements approved between mid-1988 and mid-1991 for the 36 countries that were reviewed in Schadler and others (1995), in only one of 13 countries that used the exchange rate as nominal anchor was there a currency crash during the planned duration of the program (Argentina in 1989, after the actual fiscal adjustment had fallen significantly short of target). In recent years, the experiences with IMF programs in countries such as Argentina, Bulgaria, CFA franc zone countries, Estonia, and Uruguay reveal a similar outcome.

Finally, it is important to note that in most of the recent currency crises, IMF support came only after exchange rate pegs had been abandoned, and official intervention was usually strictly limited in IMF programs. This was the case for Mexico in the tequila crisis, and for Thailand, Indonesia, the Republic of Korea, and the Philippines in the Asian crisis.

---

[66]See IMF Assessment Project (1992; p. 39). Johnson and others (1985) examined IMF-supported programs in a single year (1983), finding that a high proportion of them involved exchange rate action. However, few of them involved a change in a long-standing peg.

[67]On early warning indicators of currency crises, see Berg and Pattillo (1998), IMF (1998a, 1999), and Milesi-Ferretti and Razin (1998). On the assessment of exchange rate misalignments, see Isard and Faruqee (1998).

Appendix V   Longer-Term Prospects for Regional Exchange Rate Policy Cooperation

For regional groups of countries that have significant intraregional economic linkages, as well as diversified linkages to industrial countries, there is a natural question about the desirable degree of cooperation in their exchange rate and other related policies. The two regional groups that presently stand out in this regard are the larger economies in the Association of Southeast Asian Nations (ASEAN) group (perhaps together with some non-ASEAN, Asian economies) and the countries in Mercosur.

As discussed in the main text, because it takes time to build political consensus and develop institutional frameworks for regional cooperation on exchange rate and related policies, the possible arrangements discussed in this appendix are probably not for implementation in the relatively near term. Nevertheless, it is relevant to consider the potential for such arrangements, with a view toward possibly building the basis for their implementation in the not too distant future.

There are three main approaches to regional cooperation on exchange rate and related policies that would appear to merit consideration. One approach is a mutual exchange rate pegging arrangement (or joint float), along the lines of the Exchange Rate Mechanism (ERM) of the European Monetary System (EMS). A second and substantially more ambitious approach would be to create regional currency unions. A third approach, which is essentially an alternative to a regional currency union, is to consider adoption of an outside currency as the monetary standard for the regional group. For assessing all three approaches, the theory of optimal currency areas is relevant. The economic criteria for it to be desirable for countries to consider forming a regional currency arrangement are, in fact, essentially the same as the criteria (described in Section III of the main text) for exchange rate pegging to be a sensible policy.

Mutual Exchange Rate Pegging

In this form of arrangement, countries participating in the regional group would agree to limit fluctuations of their mutual exchange rates to within agreed bands around prescribed central parities. The central parities might be defined in terms of some formula involving only exchange rates among currencies in the group or, much more likely, they might be defined with reference to some external standard such as the currency of one of the major industrial countries or (probably preferably) an agreed basket of such currencies. Moreover, there probably would be understandings concerning mutual support and appropriate policy reactions when exchange rates reached or neared the limits of these bands. There would also be a mechanism for regional consultation on adjustments of central parities when such adjustments appeared necessary to deal with "fundamental disequilibria."

The virtues and defects of such an arrangement, and the circumstances in which it is likely to work reasonably well or relatively poorly, are illustrated by European experience with the ERM and its predecessors. In Europe, the ERM and its predecessors did help to stabilize exchange rates among the participating countries. This was particularly important because trade linkages between the participating countries (measured relative to their total trade and, especially, relative to their GDPs) were very substantial—an indication that these countries fit one of the key criteria for an optimal currency area. In contrast, intraregional trade linkages in ASEAN and Mercosur (discussed further below), while important, are significantly less so than in Europe. Also (as discussed further below), the ASEAN and Mercosur countries seem to be subject to much greater asymmetry of shocks than that which typically characterizes the situation in Europe—another indication that these regional groups do not fit particularly well the criteria for optimal currency areas. Moreover, in Europe there was a central country, Germany, whose currency formed the natural focus for efforts at regional exchange rate stabilization. There is no corresponding counterpart in either ASEAN or Mercosur. And in Europe, as the effective degree of capital market integration increased, the ERM became increasingly vulnerable to market pressures.

All of this does not necessarily argue that regional pegging arrangements would be entirely unworkable and undesirable for ASEAN or Mercosur. However, for such an arrangement to be helpful, it probably should have fairly wide bands and should contemplate the possibility of relatively frequent adjustments of central parities. In view of the substantial involvement of the key countries of ASEAN and Mercosur with global financial markets, an effort to tightly manage exchange rates through some regional mechanism, without extremely strong policy commitments and institutional support, is probably an invitation to repeated crises.

Common Currency Areas

Currency unions among independent states have been relatively rare, since they typically require tight integration along many economic and perhaps political dimensions. The most important in scale is the euro zone, which has been in operation as a common currency area only since the beginning of 1999. Other examples include the Eastern Caribbean dollar area and the CFA franc zone. In the latter example, two groups of west and central African states have for 50 years maintained a common currency pegged (with one adjustment in 1994) to the French franc (now to the euro), with the support of the French Treasury. Also, four southern African countries maintain the Common Monetary Area, in which the South African rand circulates freely in the neighboring states of Lesotho, Namibia, and Swaziland (which also issue their own currencies at par with the rand).

Economic theory and experience suggest that there is no simple answer as to whether a group of countries would benefit from a common currency. The theory of optimal currency areas describes the factors that determine whether a particular set of countries would be better off with or without a common currency.[68] These factors are similar to the criteria for choosing to peg to another currency, but with the added need to consider building regional monetary institutions and macroeconomic coordination. Creation of such institutions and the introduction of a common currency would remove the risks of speculative attack to which pegs can be subjected in the presence of high capital mobility. This appendix considers the application of optimal currency area criteria to the countries that compose Mercosur and ASEAN.

The first consideration is that countries that trade substantially with each other would benefit from a common currency, which would minimize transaction costs and disruptions due to exchange rate fluctuations. By this criterion, neither ASEAN nor Mercosur are obvious candidates for a common currency, as their share of regional trade is about one-fourth, compared to one-half for the countries of the EU or NAFTA (Table 3.2).

An important caveat to this conclusion is that this analysis is based on historical trade shares. Mercosur in particular is fairly recent, and intraregional liberalization has grown and is likely to continue to grow in both regions over time, as shown in Figure A5.1. This liberalization is likely to promote intraregional trade, as argued by Frankel and Rose (1998) and as discussed above. It is possible, moreover, that the formation of a common currency could itself strengthen trade links by reducing exchange rate swings and any resulting protectionist pressures, thereby encouraging more trade within the region. Countries with a common currency forgo the ability to adjust their nominal exchange rate. Thus, the second consideration is whether the loss of this flexibility would likely be costly, because the countries in question suffer asymmetric shocks. The evidence for Mercosur and ASEAN suggests that countries within each region suffer from dissimilar patterns of shocks. For example, Bayoumi and Eichengreen (1994) find that shocks to output in Brazil and Argentina are highly uncorrelated, suggesting that a fixed bilateral exchange rate would create serious problems with regard to stabilization of output in the two countries. Supply shocks affecting some of the ASEAN countries, in particular Indonesia, Malaysia, and Singapore, are quite similar, while those for the Philippines and Thailand are relatively asymmetric, showing lower correlation with the other countries of ASEAN.[69] In consequence, the costs of reducing flexibility implied by the adoption of common currencies could be substantial for some of the countries of Mercosur and ASEAN.

An important limitation of these studies based on historical data is that they necessarily ignore the likelihood that the correlation of shocks depends in part on the exchange arrangement. Some sources of actual output fluctuation are monetary and would be eliminated by the creation of a common currency. For example, some of the large fluctuations in the Argentina/Brazil bilateral real exchange rate have reflected divergent monetary policies and the fact that their currencies were subjected to different pres-

---

[68]The theory of optimal currency areas originated from Robert Mundell's (1961) seminal work.

[69]For other groupings of Asian countries, Bayoumi and Eichengreen (1994) and Eichengreen and Bayoumi (1999) find that the symmetry of shocks is distinctly greater.

Figure A5.1. Selected Regional Groups: Intraregional Trade
(As a share of total regional trade; annual averages)

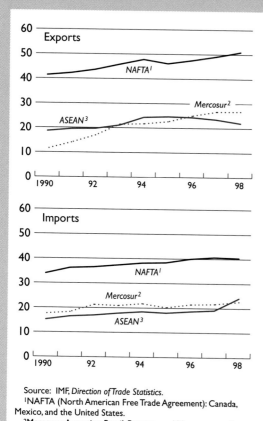

Source: IMF, *Direction of Trade Statistics.*
[1]NAFTA (North American Free Trade Agreement): Canada, Mexico, and the United States.
[2]Mercosur: Argentina, Brazil, Paraguay, and Uruguay, as well as associate members Bolivia and Chile.
[3]ASEAN (Association of Southeast Asian Nations): Cambodia, Indonesia, Lao P.D.R., Malaysia, Myanmar, Philippines, Singapore, Thailand, and Vietnam. (Brunei data not available.)

tically integrated, then demand shocks might affect both countries more symmetrically. Empirically, there is some evidence that growing trade integration leads to patterns of shocks becoming more similar over time.[71]

A further factor that influences whether a group of countries should create a common currency is the degree of internal flexibility in goods and labor markets. A fixed exchange rate regime, by eliminating the option of exchange rate adjustments, puts more pressure on adjustments of nominal wages and prices when real exchange rates become misaligned as a result of asymmetric shocks. Countries with relatively flexible wage rates and goods prices, then, would find a fixed exchange rate regime less costly. By this benchmark, the countries of ASEAN would appear to be better suited to a common currency by virtue of a relative absence of rigidities in labor and product markets. A common currency would, in contrast, place substantial pressure on labor markets in the countries of Mercosur, some of which exhibit significant inflexibility. The relatively slow decline of unemployment rates observed in particular in Argentina even after a period of strong growth suggests that much progress remains to be made.[72]

A final and important factor in considering whether to establish a common currency area is the need to strengthen regional economic institutions. A common currency area requires a substantial degree of coordination of monetary and fiscal policies, best assured in some dimensions by the creation of shared institutions, most importantly a common central bank (or coordinated system of central banks). The countries must also agree on a common monetary-policymaking process and ultimately on a common policy.

Coordination of fiscal policy will also be complex. First, some fiscal policy issues are tightly linked to monetary policy itself. In ASEAN, for example, it is common for national central banks to pursue sectoral credit growth objectives, which implicitly involve subsidies and taxes. To manage a common monetary policy it would likely be necessary that disguised fiscal activities be made explicit. Moreover, a system of fiscal transfers could be important in buffering shocks that affect the countries within the region differentially.[73] This sort of mecha-

sures stemming from the tequila crisis.[70] More generally, the structures of economies that are linked in a common currency area are sure to evolve as a result of that linkage. This integration might increase or might decrease the degree of commonality of shocks faced by the countries. If the countries became more specialized in their industrial structure they might then be subject to different industry-specific shocks. If, on the other hand, they became ver-

---

[70]Bevilaqua (1997) describes the role of macroeconomic policy, particularly inflation stabilizations, in "shocking" the Argentinean and Brazilian economies at different times. However, Eichengreen and Bayoumi (1999) find a low correlation even for shocks that they identify as supply shocks and which thus are not in principle related to monetary policy. See also Levy-Yeyati and Sturzenegger (1999), who reach similar conclusions.

[71]See Frankel and Rose (1998).
[72]Even this structural aspect of the economy may be somewhat endogenous to the exchange rate regime. Nominal prices and wages are presumably more downward-flexible now in Argentina than they were in the period before the currency board began operating.
[73]Sachs and Sala-i-Martin (1991) argue that fiscal transfers between regions of the United States are an important component of adjustment to asymmetric shocks.

nism, however, would be politically challenging to implement.

As discussed above, labor market flexibility would be important to compensate for the loss of the exchange rate as a policy tool. Although this primarily concerns internal wage flexibility and labor mobility, such flexibility would also be enhanced by agreements promoting intraregional mobility. A lack of emphasis on this issue in the run-up to the creation of the euro is widely acknowledged to have been an important omission.[74] These institutional developments would require a substantial degree of cooperation and regional solidarity.

While the costs of volatile bilateral exchange rates may be increasing with greater regional trade integration, the requirements of institutional and structural reform appear challenging for both Mercosur and ASEAN. The interdependence of the various aspects of regional integration is well illustrated by the EU, where the introduction of the euro has followed more than 40 years of initiatives leading to greater harmonization, coordination, and convergence among member countries, with greater political integration remaining a firm objective for the future. The countries of Mercosur have made substantial progress in creating independent national central banks. Progress in creating strong financial institutions, flexible labor markets, and sustainable fiscal policies is more mixed. The countries of ASEAN also have some distance to go before they can meet these requirements.[75] In both regions, it seems that regional solidarity would need to be developed in order to create a regional central bank and to abandon irrevocably national currencies and national monetary policymaking sovereignty.

Common Links to a Third Currency: "Dollar" Zones

Building regional institutions to support a regional currency is a demanding task. Indeed, existing common currency areas developed on the basis of pegs by a set of countries to a strong central currency. In the case of the euro, the deutsche mark provided a stable central currency that lent credibility to the transition to the common currency, and the Bundesbank provided a model for the European Central Bank. Yet, even with strong political consensus, the task of actually moving to EMU took many years to complete. For the currencies of the west and central

African states of the CFA franc zone, monetary policy credibility derives in important measure from their tight linkage to the French franc and the associated support of the French Treasury.[76]

Countries considering the creation of a common currency area may, therefore, consider adopting a common third currency, such as the dollar. This avoids the need to create some of the complex intraregional institutions such as a central bank and, by eliminating the exchange rate as an issue, immediately enhances the credibility of the currency area. However, countries considering such an arrangement ought to consider whether the region augmented by the country issuing the currency (e.g., the United States) is an optimal currency area. Since Argentina has already linked its currency to the U.S. dollar, the issue would not arise for that country, but it would arise for Argentina's Mercosur neighbors. The same criteria discussed above—that is, the extent to which trade shares are high and patterns of shocks are similar—apply.

Table 3.2 shows the trade shares for Mercosur including the United States and ASEAN including the United States and, alternatively, Japan. Although still low compared to the degree of trade integration of EU members prior to the introduction of the euro, these trade shares are substantially higher than those for Mercosur or ASEAN alone. Therefore, looking solely at the potential benefits would suggest that joining a larger currency area by adopting a major international currency should make the formation of a currency union more attractive.

The problem of asymmetric shocks, however, is more acute. Shocks to the United States and Japan, for example, are likely to be quite different from the shocks that impact ASEAN and Mercosur members.[77] This is illustrated by the pressures put on the de facto pegs to the dollar of Asian countries following the dollar's appreciation in 1995–97. Also, as Larrain (1999) points out, the dollar's "safe haven" character tends to cause it to appreciate during bouts of crisis in emerging market countries.

While the requirements for regional institutional and structural development are reduced under this option, others remain, and new ones are created. The

---

[74]See Eichengreen (1998).

[75]On the prospects and history of Asian economic integration, see Eichengreen and Bayoumi (1999) and Bayoumi and Mauro (1999).

[76]Central bank credibility is also enhanced by tight limits on credits to member governments and the independence of the regional central banks.

[77]Bayoumi and Eichengreen (1994) find, for example, that supply shocks in the United States are negatively correlated with supply shocks in Argentina, Paraguay, and Uruguay and only slightly positively correlated with supply shocks in Brazil, over the 1972 to 1989 period. Their results on the relationship between supply shocks in Japan and the ASEAN countries present a less clear pattern, but it is clear that the correlations are not high relative, say, to those among EU countries.

needs for labor market flexibility, fiscal policy sustainability, and financial system strength are similar to those of an autonomous common currency area. Moreover, the adoption of an outside currency (unlike a peg) implies a transfer of seigniorage to the country that issues the currency, unless some sharing arrangement can be made with that country.

A potentially more serious problem is that the lender of last resort function of central banks of the region would be impaired. Problems at individual financial institutions could still be handled if the central bank (or some other government agency) had resources beyond the backing required for the currency or could draw on established lines of credit with international banks. However, the authorities would lose the ability to provide potentially unlimited liquidity in response to a sudden generalized shift from bank deposits to currency throughout the entire system. This loss of flexibility should not be exaggerated, however. In any exchange rate regime, the injection of liquidity into the banking system to keep it from defaulting on depositors may only lead to greater pressure on foreign exchange reserves or on the exchange rate, and so an emerging market central bank would in any case encounter limits to its effectiveness in dealing with crises. Also, the need for a systemic lender of last resort might be ameliorated by the presence of large and solid foreign banks in the domestic market both because those banks might indirectly obtain support from their head offices, and because depositors' confidence in the financial backing of those institutions might be higher.

Of course, countries could choose to anchor their exchange rate policy to an outside currency without adopting that currency, as in a regional pegged regime such as a currency board. This is, in effect, a variant of the previous option: if regional groups adopt their own common currency, the region as a group may choose to peg to an external currency. But it would be a mistake to think that the choice of a peg to an outside currency would greatly reduce the requirements for operating the common currency. For a group of countries without their own strong central currency (which is the case for both ASEAN and Mercosur) the requirements for coordinating policy across countries would remain substantial, and the credibility gains from an adjustable peg would likely be limited. Such a peg would be subject to speculative attack unless the commitment to supporting policies, including the coordination among members of the currency union, was viewed as strongly credible.

Conclusion on Regional Currency Arrangements

The successful experience of NAFTA shows that regional trading areas do not have to share a common currency. However, closer forms of integration, largely driven by political rather than economic forces, may be incompatible with flexible rates. In Europe, many policymakers came to a strong belief that further integration required monetary union. Eichengreen (1998) suggests how to reconcile these different experiences in order to draw lessons for prospective currency unions such as Mercosur and ASEAN. Where integration is at most a customs union or a free trade agreement, as with NAFTA, exchange rates that float intraregionally appear much more sustainable. In contrast, freely fluctuating exchange rates may create intolerable political strains in cases where integration is to extend to the harmonization in national policies across a wide array of economic and social issues, requiring substantial transfer of policymaking authority to supranational bodies. Whether Mercosur or ASEAN will, in the future, wish to consider a strong form of exchange rate and monetary policy cooperation, including possibly a common currency, thus depends in large part on how far they intend to pursue the project of regional economic and political integration.

If these countries want to consider fuller integration, the challenges for the creation of a common currency are substantial, as discussed above. All of this suggests that these regions should not base the decision of whether or not to adopt a common currency on short-run considerations. Over time, many of the obstacles to a common currency area could be overcome if there is the political will to do so. Moreover, some of the steps required to form a common currency area may be ends in themselves for the countries involved. Enhanced labor market flexibility, sustainable fiscal policies, and monetary policies that achieve convergence to low inflation, for example, would be valuable even in the absence of a currency union. Even tighter political cooperation within the region may be an objective in its own right. To the extent that it is, the goal of a common currency may provide an instrument to help achieve these other objectives. The difficulties should not be underestimated, but if the countries in the region desire integration beyond the level of a customs union and work toward that end, a common currency would eventually be a viable option.

Appendix VI Summing Up by the Acting Chairman

Exchange Rate Regimes in an Increasingly Integrated World Economy[78]

Executive Directors welcomed the opportunity to revisit the question of choice of exchange rate regime—a topic central to the Fund's mandate and to the international monetary system. They considered that the diversity of exchange rate regimes present in the international monetary system was likely to continue, and emphasized that no single exchange rate arrangement was appropriate for all countries, or in all circumstances. Many factors properly enter into the choice of regime. These primarily include economic criteria, such as the extent of trade with partner countries, symmetry of shocks, and the existence of institutions and markets able to handle exchange rate fluctuations. But they may also include political considerations, such as a desire to proceed with regional integration.

Many Directors considered that the widespread liberalization and expansion of capital movements had made it more difficult to sustain pegged rates and thus, for a significant number of countries, had tended to shift the balance of advantage in favor of adopting more flexible regimes. However, Directors emphasized that exchange rate flexibility was not a soft option and that exchange rate and macroeconomic stability required the pursuit of stability-oriented policies. They also acknowledged that very constraining pegs—such as currency boards—when supported by macroeconomic policy discipline, could also be credible and sustainable.

Directors agreed that, whether exchange rates were pegged or flexible, greater capital mobility had exposed domestic financial institutions to increased pressures in the form of interest rate or exchange rate fluctuations, which underlined the essential need to strengthen financial systems. Directors also emphasized the contribution that other factors—such as corporate financial structures and transparency in public decision making—could make to the effective operation of exchange rate regimes, both pegged and flexible. They also pointed to the need to encourage the development of futures and forward markets that would make it easier to hedge against exchange rate movements.

Directors considered the regime likely to prevail in the medium term among the three major currency blocs centered on the dollar, the euro, and the yen. These currencies would likely continue to anchor the international monetary system, and thus affect significantly the environment in which other countries' exchange rate choices are made. The launch of the euro at the beginning of 1999 was a major event for the international monetary system. Directors did not believe that it would change the existing system of flexibility among the exchange rates of the key currencies, nor did most Directors consider that there was any evidence that the euro would fluctuate significantly less against the dollar and the yen than had been the case for a basket of its component currencies. Directors considered it likely, as well as appropriate, that the largest countries would focus their monetary policies primarily on domestic considerations, especially to ensure domestic price stability, rather than target a particular level for their currency's exchange rate. While recognizing the constraints on the effectiveness of remedial official action, Directors nonetheless emphasized that large misalignments and volatility in these currencies' values were a cause for concern, in particular for small, open commodity-exporting countries. They stressed that the Fund should remain vigilant and ensure that externalities arising from the macroeconomic and structural policies of major currency countries are fully taken into account in the surveillance process. A few Directors pointed to the potential benefits of coordinated exchange rate management to further help limit short-term exchange rate volatility.

For the smaller, more open economies, and especially those with limited involvement in global capital markets, Directors considered that a peg to one or another of the major currencies, or to the currency of

---

[78]The IMF Executive Board discussed the paper on Exchange Rate Regimes in an Integrated World Economy on September 21, 1999. This summing up represents the Acting Chairman's summary of the Board discussion.

a dominant trading partner (where one existed), or to a basket of currencies would likely continue to be the preferred course. For such countries with both disciplined fiscal policies and no reason to exercise an independent monetary policy, a peg could be credible and hence unlikely to suffer from speculative attacks.

For a significant number of other economies, however—notably medium-sized industrial and emerging market economies—many Directors considered that the heightened policy requirements imposed by the liberalization of capital flows had increased the difficulty of defending pegged rates. As a result, they perceived a tendency toward either more flexible arrangements or more constraining, and hence more credible, exchange rate systems—including the adoption of a currency board, "dollarization," or monetary union involving a move to a common currency. Directors noted that this tendency had been evident among industrial countries. A number of medium-sized countries have flexible exchange rates, while others, particularly in Europe, have replaced national currencies with the euro. Directors observed that this tendency had been less evident among developing countries, in part because for many of them capital mobility is still restricted.

Most Directors agreed that for many of the so-called "emerging market economies," which by definition have access to international capital markets, a substantial degree of exchange rate flexibility is desirable. However, they did not consider that freely flexible exchange rates would be a viable option for all such economies, and recognized that in practice, many would want to use intervention and domestic monetary policy to guide exchange rate movements. Such arrangements could be loosely managed or they could be less flexible, including a crawling peg or band. Directors also noted that pegged rates (or active crawling pegs) could be quite appropriate in other circumstances, such as stabilization from high inflation.

Directors noted that under a flexible regime, a credible alternative framework to the exchange rate peg is needed to provide a nominal anchor. A number of Directors believed that inflation targeting could provide such a transparent and credible framework for developing countries, just as it does for several industrial countries. Some Directors stressed that the preconditions for successful inflation targeting, which included the independence of the central bank from fiscal or political pressures, a reliable framework for forecasting inflation, and the ability to move interest rates to attain the inflation objectives, were not satisfied in many developing countries. In the view of these Directors, these considerations might reinforce the case for countries adopting a pegged arrangement.

In considering whether regional exchange rate arrangements might be appropriate for groups of developing countries, Directors focused on two regions, Mercosur and ASEAN. Some Directors considered that in neither of these cases did the countries in the region form an optimum currency area, since some of them had different economic structures and faced different shocks. They stressed that not only economic similarity, but also political solidarity, was necessary to make a monetary union work. On this criterion, both Mercosur and ASEAN probably needed to progress further in their commitment to regional institutions before contemplating monetary union. Other Directors pointed out that the ongoing macroeconomic stabilization and structural reforms in countries in these areas should help achieve faster progress toward regional groupings.

Directors also considered the issue of exchange rate policy advice in the context of Fund-supported programs, noting that past practice has been not to dictate the member's exchange rate arrangement, but rather to assess the consistency of economic policies with the regime chosen. Directors noted that in recent programs with Asian crisis countries and with Mexico, large-scale Fund assistance had been provided after an exit from unsustainable official or de facto pegs or bands, rather than in defense of an exchange rate commitment. Nevertheless, the Fund had at times provided financing to countries with pegged exchange rates that were forced to abandon them during the life of the program, two recent examples being Brazil and Russia.

Directors recognized that countries' choices regarding exchange rate regimes could be difficult and sensitive. While taking due account of these difficulties, the Fund should offer its own views to assist national authorities in their policy deliberations. In particular, the Fund should seek to ensure that countries' policies and circumstances are consistent with their choice of exchange rate regime. In some cases where the issue arose, this would require the Fund to offer advice on an appropriate strategy for exiting a fixed exchange rate regime. Directors agreed that the Fund should not provide large-scale assistance to countries intervening heavily to support an exchange rate peg, if this peg is inconsistent with the underlying policies. In this context, some Directors stressed the importance of supporting institutional arrangements that can help make domestic policy commitments more credible.

In closing the discussion, Directors agreed that there were no simple answers to the question of the choice of exchange rate regime. Depending on a country's starting point in terms of inflation history, economic structure, and political commitment, various arrangements ranging from a hard peg to a high degree of exchange rate flexibility could be considered. Whatever exchange rate regime was adopted, however, its consistency with underlying macroeconomic policies was essential. Directors further noted that the Fund should continue to exercise firm surveillance over the exchange rate systems of members and should strive to provide clear advice to members on their choice of exchange rate systems. Directors agreed that the Board needed periodically to revisit country experience and the Fund's policy advice in this important area, which was central to its mandate.

Exchange Rate Regimes in an Increasingly Integrated World Economy—Further Considerations[79]

Executive Directors reaffirmed the main conclusions of their previous discussion as summarized in the Acting Chairman's summing up of Executive Board Meeting 99/107 (9/21/99). In their further discussion, Directors noted that the choice of an exchange rate regime assumed particular importance for both advanced and emerging market economies with substantial and growing involvement in world capital markets. They emphasized the complexities involved in judging precisely at which point an economy is sufficiently integrated with world capital markets to drive the country's choice of exchange rate regime toward one or the other end of the spectrum of options: namely a hard peg, which necessarily implies that monetary policy be made almost entirely subservient to the maintenance of the peg, or a regime of substantial exchange rate flexibility, which, to be stable, requires that a nominal anchor other than the exchange rate be provided. A number of Directors also stated that a spectrum of viable alternative options existed between the two extreme exchange rate regimes. Another option that is available—to maintain or even reinforce controls of capital movements if some monetary independence is to be pursued together with exchange rate pegging arrangements—was seen by a number of Directors as not sustainable in the medium term.

With respect to countries that opt for a fixed exchange rate regime, Directors emphasized that institutional constraints that bind monetary policy to maintenance of the parity (such as the very hard pegs implied by arrangements of the currency board type), together with fiscal discipline, are important

in ensuring the credibility and stability of the regime, and increasingly so with the degree of participation in world financial markets.

As for other supporting policies, Directors emphasized that countries should avoid de jure or de facto pegs not adequately supported by other elements of economic policy and institutions; in particular, there should be reasonable assurance that the authorities are able and willing to adjust interest rates in order to defend the peg in cases of stress without threatening massive insolvencies or a collapse in employment and output.

With respect to flexible exchange rate regimes, Directors stressed that flexibility still requires that macroeconomic policies be coherent with the regime, and that macroeconomic stability still requires strong macroeconomic policies. They emphasized the importance of providing an alternative nominal anchor to the exchange rate, and noted that inflation targeting would be one such alternative. A few Directors noted, however, that inflation targeting is a demanding framework. Directors encouraged the staff to continue its work on the effectiveness and appropriate form of inflation targeting policies, as well as on other policies that could provide a nominal anchor for the economy. They looked forward to considering, in the near term, the implications of inflation targeting for Fund conditionality. In addition, for emerging market countries that adopt more flexible exchange rate regimes, most Directors wished to reaffirm their earlier conclusion that, in general, it would be appropriate to limit excessive fluctuations not only through adjustment in domestic monetary policy, but also through intervention.

A number of Directors noted that countries with extensive capital controls appear to have had some more latitude than countries with open capital and trade accounts for using monetary policy for domestic objectives while maintaining an exchange rate peg, particularly in the short run. Directors recognized, however, that such controls are a source of distortions that are often costly and detrimental to growth in the long run. Directors thought that it would be in the longer-term interest of emerging market economies to move toward a more open capital account. They emphasized that such moves toward liberalization must be undertaken in a safe and orderly manner, with due attention being paid to the strengthening of macroeconomic policies and of the domestic financial system.

Turning to the use of pegging arrangements, notably of the active crawling peg variety, Directors agreed that they could prove a useful tool in stabilizing from high inflation. However, Directors noted that it was important to recognize the need for an exit strategy and prepare for it early enough to avoid the scheme becoming unsustainable and collapsing,

---

[79]The IMF Executive Board discussed the paper on *Exchange Rate Regimes in an Increasingly Integrated World Economy—Further Considerations* on November 15, 1999. This summing up represents the Acting Chairman's summary of the Board discussion.

leading to a renewal of inflation and serious employment problems. Such an exit would involve a move to a flexible regime, or possibly to a peg at a different level. Ideally, the transition to a new exchange regime should take place during a period of relative calm in exchange markets. Directors stressed that the Fund should continue to play an important role in providing members with timely and candid advice on the appropriate exit strategy. They emphasized the critical importance of a robust financial system and strong prudential regulations and supervision in advance of the exit. Directors encouraged the staff to collaborate at an early stage with countries using pegs in designing such exit strategies.

Directors emphasized that, in its approach to issues dealing with exchange rate regimes, the Fund must take into account the provisions in the Articles of Agreement that it is for members to choose their exchange rate arrangements. They stressed that the Fund should continue, in the context of Article IV consultations, to discuss with country authorities the requirements for making a chosen exchange rate regime function reasonably well in the particular circumstances of that country and to actively advise on the suitability of the exchange rate regime. They agreed that in program cases, renewed emphasis should be placed on the overall consistency of the member's economic policies, including its choice of exchange rate regime, and that the Fund should continue to avoid providing its financial support to defend an unsustainable peg, or an unsustainable exchange rate in the context of a managed float.

Directors invited the staff to continue to monitor, debate, and analyze the accumulating experience of members with exchange rate regimes in the context of open capital markets, so as to enable the Fund to continually improve its policy advice and the effectiveness of its financial support to its members.

References

Aghevli, Bijan B., Mohsin S. Khan, and Peter Montiel, 1991, *Exchange Rate Policy in Developing Countries: Some Analytical Issues,* IMF Occasional Paper 78 (Washington: International Monetary Fund).

Argy, Victor, 1990, "Choice of Exchange Rate Regime for a Smaller Economy: A Survey of Some Key Issues," in *Choosing an Exchange Rate Regime: The Challenge for Smaller Industrial Countries*, ed. by Victor Argy and Paul De Grauwe (Washington: International Monetary Fund), pp. 6–81.

Ariyoshi, Akira, Karl Habermeier, Bernard Laurens, Inci Ötker-Robe, Jorge Iván Canales-Kriljenko, and Andrei Kirilenko, 2000, *Capital Controls: Country Experiences with Their Use and Liberalization,* IMF Occasional Paper 190 (Washington: International Monetary Fund).

Balassa, Bela, 1964, "The Purchasing-Power Parity Doctrine: A Reappraisal," *Journal of Political Economy*, Vol. 72, No. 6, pp. 584–96.

Baliño, Tomás, Charles Enoch, and others, 1997, *Currency Board Arrangements: Issues and Experiences,* IMF Occasional Paper 151 (Washington: International Monetary Fund).

Bayoumi, Tamim A., and Barry Eichengreen, 1994, *One Money or Many?: Analyzing the Prospects for Monetary Unification in Various Parts of the World* (mimeo, International Finance Section, Department of Economics, Princeton University).

Bayoumi, Tamim A., and Paolo Mauro, 1999, "The Suitability of ASEAN for a Regional Currency Arrangement," IMF Working Paper 99/162 (Washington: International Monetary Fund).

Bénassy-Quéré, Agnès, Benoît Mojon, and Jean Pisani-Ferry, 1997, "The Euro and Exchange Rate Stability," in *EMU and the International Monetary System,* ed. by Paul R. Masson, Thomas H. Krueger, and Bart G. Turtelboom (Washington: International Monetary Fund), pp. 397–417.

Bennett, Adam, 1995, "Currency Board: Issues and Experiences," *Finance & Development*, Vol. 32 (September), pp. 39–42.

Berg, Andrew, and Catherine Pattillo, 1998, "Are Currency Crises Predictable? A Test," IMF Working Paper 98/154 (Washington: International Monetary Fund).

Bernanke, Ben, Thomas Laubach, Frederic S. Mishkin, and Adam Posen, 1999, *Inflation Targeting: Lessons from the International Experience* (Princeton, New Jersey: Princeton University Press).

Bevilaqua, Afonso S., 1997, "Macroeconomic Coordination and Commercial Integration in Mercosur," *Texto Para Discussao No. 378*, Departmento de Economía.

Calvo, Guillermo A., and Carlos A. Végh, 1999, "Inflation Stabilization and BOP Crises in Developing Countries," NBER Working Paper 6925 (Cambridge, Massachusetts: National Bureau of Economic Research).

Carstens, Agustin G., and Alejandro M. Werner, 1999, "Mexico's Monetary Policy Framework Under a Floating Exchange Rate Regime," *Serie Documentos de Investigacion No. 9905*, Bank of Mexico (May), available via Internet at the web page: www.banxico.org.mx/public-html/inveco/doctas/docinves/document.html.

Cohen, Daniel, 1997, "How Will the Euro Behave?" in *EMU and the International Monetary System,* ed. by Paul R. Masson, Thomas H. Krueger, and Bart G. Turtelboom (Washington: International Monetary Fund), pp. 397–417.

Commission of the European Communities, 1990, "One Market, One Money: An Evaluation of the Potential Benefits and Costs of Forming an Economic and Monetary Union," *European Economy*, No. 44 (Brussels: Commission of the European Communities).

Cottarelli, Carlo, and Curzio Giannini, 1997, *Credibility Without Rules? Monetary Frameworks in the Post-Bretton Woods Era,* IMF Occasional Paper 154 (Washington: International Monetary Fund).

Crockett, Andrew, and Morris Goldstein, 1987, *Strengthening the International Monetary System: Exchange Rates, Surveillance, and Objective Indicators,* IMF Occasional Paper 50 (Washington: International Monetary Fund).

Dell'Ariccia, Giovanni, 1998, "Exchange Rate Fluctuations and Trade Flows: Evidence from the European Union," IMF Working Paper 98/107 (Washington: International Monetary Fund).

Edison, Hali J., and Michael Melvin, 1990, "The Determinants and Implications of the Choice of Exchange Rate Regime," in *Monetary Policy for a Volatile Global Economy,* ed. by William S. Haraf and Thomas D. Willett (Washington: AEI Press).

Edwards, Sebastian, and Miguel Savastano, 1998, "Exchange Rates in Emerging Economies: What Do We Know? What Do We Need to Know?" NBER Working Paper 7228 (Cambridge, Massachusetts: National Bureau of Economic Research).

——, 1998, "The Morning After: The Mexican Peso in the Aftermath of the 1994 Currency Crisis," NBER Working Paper 6516 (Cambridge, Massachusetts: National Bureau of Economic Research).

Eichengreen, Barry, 1997, "European Monetary Unification and International Monetary Cooperation," Cider Working Paper C97–091 (Berkeley: Center for International and Development Economics Research, University of California).

——, 1998, "Does Mercosur Need a Single Currency?" NBER Working Paper 6821 (Cambridge, Massachusetts: National Bureau of Economic Research).

Eichengreen, Barry, and Tamim Bayoumi, 1999, "Is Asia an Optimal Currency Area? Can It Become One? Regional, Global and Historical Perspectives on Asian Monetary Relations," in *Exchange Rate Policies in Emerging Asian Countries*, ed. by Stefan Collignon, Jean Pisani-Ferry, and Yung Chul Park (London; New York: Routledge).

Eichengreen, Barry, Paul Masson, Hugh Bredenkamp, Barry Johnston, Javier Hamann, Esteban Jadresic, and Inci Ötker, 1998, *Exit Strategies: Policy Options for Countries Seeking Greater Exchange Rate Flexibility,* IMF Occasional Paper 168 (Washington: International Monetary Fund).

Eichengreen, Barry, Paul Masson, Miguel Savastano, and Sunil Sharma, 1999, "Transition Strategies and Nominal Anchors on the Road to Greater Exchange Rate Flexibility," *Essays in International Finance,* No. 213 (Princeton, New Jersey: Princeton University Press).

Eichengreen, Barry, Michael Mussa, Giovanni Dell'Ariccia, Enrica Detragiache, Gian Maria Milesi-Ferretti, and Andrew Tweedie, 1999, "Liberalizing Capital Movements: Some Analytical Issues," *Economic Issues 17* (Washington: International Monetary Fund).

Feldstein, Martin, 1988, "Distinguished Lecture on Economics in Government: Thinking About International Economic Coordination," *Journal of Economic Perspectives*, Vol. 2, pp. 3–13.

Flood, Robert, and Andrew Rose, 1995, "Fixing Exchange Rates: A Virtual Quest for Fundamentals," *Journal of Monetary Economics*, Vol. 36 (August), pp. 3–37.

Frankel, Jeffrey A., 1997, *Regional Trading Blocs in the World Economic System* (Washington: Institute for International Economics).

——, 1999, "No Single Currency Regime Is Right for All Countries or at All Times," *Essays in International Finance*, No. 215 (Princeton, New Jersey: Princeton University).

Frankel, Jeffrey A., and Andrew Rose, 1998, "The Endogeneity of the Optimum Currency Area Criteria," NBER Working Paper 5700 (Cambridge, Massachusetts: National Bureau of Economic Research).

——, 1996, "Currency Crashes in Emerging Markets: Empirical Indicators," NBER Working Paper 5437 (Cambridge, Massachusetts: National Bureau of Economic Research).

Frankel, Jeffrey A., and Shang-Jin Wei, 1993, "Trade Blocs and Currency Blocs," NBER Working Paper 4335 (Cambridge, Massachusetts: National Bureau of Economic Research).

Gagnon, Joseph E., 1993, "Exchange Rate Variability and the Level of International Trade," *Journal of International Economics*, Vol. 34 (May), pp. 269–87.

Genberg, Hans, 1989, "Exchange Rate Management and Macroeconomic Policy: A National Perspective," *Scandinavian Journal of Economics*, Vol. 91, No. 2, pp. 439–69.

Ghosh, Atish R., Anne-Marie Gulde, Jonathan D. Ostry, and Holger C. Wolf, 1995, "Does the Nominal Exchange Rate Regime Matter?" IMF Working Paper 95/121 (Washington: International Monetary Fund).

Gulde, Anne-Marie, Juha Kähkönen, and Peter Keller, 2000, "Pros and Cons of Currency Board Arrangements in the Lead-Up to EU Accession and Participation in the Euro Zone," IMF Policy Discussion Paper 00/1 (Washington: International Monetary Fund).

Hausman, Ricardo, Michael Gavin, Carmen Páges-Serra, and Ernesto H. Stein, 1999, "Financial Turmoil and the Choice of Exchange Rate Regime," Working Paper 400 (Washington: Inter-American Development Bank), available via Internet at the web page: www.iadb.org/oce/33.cfm?code=1.

Hoffmaister, Alexander W., Jorge E. Roldós, and Peter Wickham, 1998, "Macroeconomic Fluctuations in Sub-Saharan Africa," *Staff Papers*, International Monetary Fund, Vol. 45 (March), pp. 132–60.

International Monetary Fund, 1984, *Exchange Rate Volatility and World Trade: A Study by the Research Department,* IMF Occasional Paper 28 (Washington: International Monetary Fund).

——, 1995a, *International Capital Markets Report* (August).

——, 1995b, *Issues in International Exchange and Payment Systems* (April).

——, 1995c, *World Economic Outlook* (May).

——, 1996, *World Economic Outlook* (October).

——, 1997, *World Economic Outlook* (October).

——, 1998a, *World Economic Outlook* (May).

——, 1998b, *World Economic Outlook and International Capital Markets: Interim Assessment* (December).

——, 1999, *World Economic Outlook* (May).

IMF Assessment Project, 1992, *IMF Conditionality 1980–91* (Arlington, Virginia: Alexis de Tocqueville Institution).

Isard, Peter, 1995, *Exchange Rate Economics* (Cambridge; New York: Cambridge University Press).

Isard, Peter, and Hamid Faruqee, eds., 1998, *Exchange Rate Assessment: Extensions of the Macroeconomic Balance Approach,* IMF Occasional Paper 167 (Washington: International Monetary Fund).

Isard, Peter, and Michael Mussa, 1998, "A Methodology for Exchange Rate Assessment," in *Exchange Rate Assessment: Extensions of the Macroeconomic Balance Approach,* ed. by Peter Isard and Hamid Faruqee, IMF Occasional Paper 167 (Washington: International Monetary Fund).

Isard, Peter, and Steven Symansky, 1996, "Long-Run Movements in Real Exchange Rates," in *Exchange Rate Movements and Their Impact on Trade and Investment in the APEC Region,* by Takatoshi Ito, Peter Isard, Steven Symanski, and Tamim Bayoumi, IMF Occasional Paper 145 (Washington: International Monetary Fund).

Ito, Takatoshi, Peter Isard, Steven Symansky, and Tamim Bayoumi, 1996, *Exchange Rate Movements and Their Impact on Trade and Investment in the APEC Region,* IMF Occasional Paper 145 (Washington: International Monetary Fund).

Johnson, G.G., and others, 1985, *Formulation of Exchange Rate Policies in Adjustment Programs,* IMF Occasional Paper 36 (Washington: International Monetary Fund).

Larrain, Felipe, 1999, "Going Green," *Worldlink Magazine* (May-June), available via Internet at the web page: http://www.worldlink.co.uk/articles/05051999175314/12.htm.

Levy-Yeyati, Eduardo, and Federico Sturzenegger, 1999, "The Euro and Latin America III: Is EMU a Blueprint for Mercosur?" (unpublished; Business School, Universidad Torcuato De Tella), available via Internet at the web page: www.utdt.edu/~fsturzen/publications.htm.

Masson, Paul, 1999, "Monetary and Exchange Rate Policy of Transition Economies of Central and Eastern Europe After the Launch of EMU," IMF Policy Discussion Paper 99/5 (Washington: International Monetary Fund).

Masson, Paul, Miguel Savastano, and Sunil Sharma, 1997, "The Scope for Inflation Targeting in Developing Countries," IMF Working Paper 97/130 (Washington: International Monetary Fund).

McKinnon, Ronald I., 1996, "Monetary and Exchange-Rate Policies for International Financial Mobility: A Proposal," in *The Rules of the Game*: *International Money and Exchange Rates,* ed. by Ronald I. McKinnon (Cambridge, Massachusetts: MIT Press).

McKinnon, Ronald I., 1999, "The East Asian Dollar Standard, Life After Death?" Working Paper 99–017 (Stanford University). Available via Internet at the webpage:www.econ.stanford.edu/faculty/workp/index.html.

Milesi-Ferretti, Gian Maria, and Assaf Razin, 1998, "Current Account Reversals and Currency Crises: Empirical Regularities," IMF Working Paper 98/89 (Washington: International Monetary Fund).

Mundell, Robert A., 1961, "A Theory of Optimum Currency Areas," *American Economic Review,* Vol. 51, No. 4, pp. 657–65.

Mussa, Michael, and Miguel Savastano, 1999, "The IMF Approach to Economic Stabilization," IMF Working Paper 99/104 (Washington: International Monetary Fund).

Mussa, Michael, Alexander Swoboda, Jeromin Zettelmeyer, and Olivier Jeanne, 1999, "Moderating Fluctuations in Capital Flows to Emerging Market Economies" (mimeo, paper presented at the Conference on Key Issues in Reform of the International Monetary and Financial System, International Monetary Fund, May 28–29).

Mussa, Michael, Morris Goldstein, Peter B. Clark, Donald J. Mathieson, and Tamim Bayoumi, 1994, *Improving the International Monetary System: Constraints and Possibilities,* IMF Occasional Paper 116 (Washington: International Monetary Fund).

Obstfeld, Maurice, 1995a, ""International Currency Experience: New Lessons and Lessons Relearned," *Brookings Papers on Economic Activity*, No. 1, pp. 119–211.

_____, 1995b, "International Capital Mobility in the 1990s," in *Understanding Interdependence: The Macroeconomics of the Open Economy*, ed. by Peter B. Kenen (Princeton, New Jersey: Princeton University Press).

Obstfeld, Maurice, and Kenneth Rogoff, 1995, "The Mirage of Fixed Exchange Rates," *Journal of Economic Perspectives*, Vol. 9, No. 4, pp. 73–96.

Ohno, Kenichi, 1999, "Exchange Rate Management in Developing Asia: A Reassessment of the Precrisis Soft-Dollar Zone," Asian Development Bank Working Paper (Manila, Philippines: Asian Development Bank).

Rubin, Robert E., 1999, "Remarks on Reform of the International Financial Architecture to the School of Advance International Studies" (April), available via Internet at the web page: http://www.treas.gov/press/releases/99arch.htm#april.

Sachs, Jeffrey, and Xavier Sala-i-Martin, 1991, "Fiscal Federalism and Optimum Currency Areas: Evidence for Europe from the United States," NBER Working Paper 3855 (Cambridge, Massachusetts: National Bureau of Economic Research).

Samuelson, Paul A., 1964, "Theoretical Notes on Trade Problems," *Review of Economics and Statistics*, Vol. 46, No. 2, pp. 145–54.

Schadler, Susan, and others, 1995, *IMF Conditionality: Experience Under Stand-By and Extended Arrangements,* IMF Occasional Paper 128 (Washington: International Monetary Fund).

Sterne, Gabriel, 1999, "The Use of Explicit Targets for Monetary Policy: Practical Experiences of 91 Economies in the 1990s," *The Bank of England Quarterly Bulletin*, Vol. 39, No. 3 (August), pp. 272–81.

Swoboda, Alexander K., 1986, "Credibility and Viability in International Monetary Arrangements," *Finance & Development*, Vol. 23 (September), pp. 15–18.

Turnovsky, Stephen J., 1982, "Determination of the Optimal Currency Basket: A Macroeconomic Analysis," *Journal of International Economics*, Vol. 12 (May), pp. 333–54.

Wickham, Peter, 1985, "Choice of Exchange Rate Regime in Developing Countries: A Survey of the Literature," *Staff Papers*, International Monetary Fund, Vol. 32 (June), pp. 248–88.

Williamson, John, 1985, *The Exchange Rate System* (Washington: Institute for International Economics).

_____, 1994, *Estimating Equilibrium Exchange Rates* (Washington: Institute for International Economics).

_____, 1995, "What Role for Currency Boards?" *Policy Analyses in International Economics*, No. 40 (Washington: Institute for International Economics).

_____, and Marcus Miller, 1987, "Targets and Indicators: A Blueprint for the International Coordination of Macroeconomic Policy," *Policy Analyses in International Economics,* No. 22 (Washington: Institute for International Economics).

World Bank, 1997, *Private Capital Flows to Developing Countries* (Oxford: Oxford University Press).